SLEEPERS

IN SEARCH OF
LOST OLD MASTERS

*To the de Ungers,
Father and son...
in awe of an outstanding
collection.*

SLEEPERS

IN SEARCH OF
LOST OLD MASTERS

Philip Mould

*With
kind regards and thanks*

Philip Mould

FOURTH ESTATE · London

First published in Great Britain in 1995 by
Fourth Estate Limited
6 Salem Road
London W2 4BU

Copyright © 1995 by Philip Mould

3 5 7 9 10 8 6 4 2

The right of Philip Mould to be identified as the author of this work
has been asserted by him in accordance with the Copyright, Designs
and Patents Act 1988.

A catalogue record of this book is available from the British Library.

ISBN 1–85702–218–1

Typeset by
Rowland Phototypesetting Ltd,
Bury St Edmunds, Suffolk
Printed in Great Britain by
Butler & Tanner Ltd,
Frome and London

To Catherine, for her love, criticism, and endurance

Contents

Acknowledgements

I owe a considerable debt to Charles Daggett, whose experience as an art dealer and writer was offered unstintingly in reacting to the manuscript. Any faults or errors are entirely my own, but his sage advice and flair have helped me greatly. This book would have been impossible without the tremendous participation of those who feature. Not only did they give me their time, but they bared their thoughts, checked facts, found photographs, and allowed me, above all, to purloin their experiences. I cannot thank them enough. I would also like to thank Sarah Beales for the quality of her research and analysis; Caroline Higgins, and latterly Caroline Cann, for translating and arduously processing my writing; and finally my brilliant editor, Jane Carr, for her ruthless queries and constant encouragement.

The author and publisher are grateful to the following for permission to reproduce illustrations: Lloyd's of London; Christie's; J. Paul Getty Museum, Malibu, California; The Royal Collection; Sotheby's; National Portrait Gallery; Stadelsches Kunstinstitut.

Introduction

A SLEEPER IS AN object, normally a picture, that passes unrecognised through an auction room into the ownership of a buyer who realises its true identity and real value. As most works of art make their first appearance in the market place at auction, this is not an uncommon phenomenon. Almost all of the stories in this book revolve around auctions, and it may be that the reader will form the impression that a certain degree of incompetence exists amongst those who write the catalogues. This is very rarely the case. An extremely high level of expertise exists in the London and New York auction houses, as well as among many of the country auctioneers – an annoying amount, in fact, for the opportunity-hunting dealer. Although errors do sometimes occur, for the most part experts will spot the potential of a piece and come up with a correct attribution and estimation of value. In some respects this is a remarkable testament to the abilities of those who, under great pressure of time, have to sort through many hundreds of items a week, as well as offering constant judgements to the general public on pictures 'over the counter' and elsewhere.

I have written this book for two reasons. I am often enraptured by my business, and know of nothing that could offer such regular excitement and fulfilment in so tangible a form as the finding and buying of unrecognised or lost works. It offers all the ingredients for high adventure: risk, drama, uncertainty, endeavour, fulfilment and, occasionally, substantial reward. I love talking about my business, although some will scold me for doing so. All too commonly discoveries are reported in the press in rather perfunctory, sensationalist terms: the initial, often indifferent perception of an object by the vendor, its then realised price, the object's true identity, and a couple of lines of appropriate, but often crass-sounding reaction. This leaves out so much: the professional and human drama, insight into the mindset which fortune favours, the indecision which can rack the finder, the critical work of the restorer, and the problems of then getting the world to believe you. Thanks to the enormous generosity of those who have talked to me, often reluctantly at first, I now hope to make the record more complete.

I also find myself part of a new generation of art dealers in a hugely evolved market. We now have to live with the eclipsing presence of the international auction houses, commercial giants whose reputation, not to mention their publicity and marketing budgets, cast a dauntingly competitive shadow over the dealer, who in many instances is supplied by them. It is no good pretending they do not exist. But the role of the efficient dealer is every bit as valid as it was when they were not so omnipresent. The huge volume of works that pass through the auctioneers' hands, in their capacity as agents, does not allow them to dwell on each individual item in quite the same way as a selective dealer with his specific and containable stock. The expertise and academic skill of many of my friends and acquaintances in the auction world is formidable. But the reason we buy from them is that we can often add that crucial bit extra, and then justify a fair price. This book describes the more dramatic examples of something we do daily in an attempt to supply our customers with things they ask for, and to which we are happy, as principals, to attach our reputations. If the auctioneers became dealers – and many of them do – they would strive to do the same.

My regret is that there are many stories, and many other dealers, which I have been unable to include. The necessities of this book require certain choices, inclusions and omissions for the sake of balance. This book is in no way a round-up of all the main discoveries in the last ten years, nor does it seek to be. I have instead attempted to explain and illustrate some of the main types of discovery that I have encountered, or heard about, and which represent what I see as the high points of our business. The account is therefore bound to be subject to personal view and experience. Nor does it dwell on the failures, the soured hunches, which feature all too commonly in the business and make the successes more sweet.

In many instances I have attempted to amplify stories that have been recounted to me, in order to explain the sensations and considerations that assail a dealer or auctioneer at the point of discovery, decision and commitment. I have attempted strenuously, in every such instance, to graft what I know to be my own reactions in that situation on to those of the discoverer. But there is always a risk of attributing thoughts and actions to people with which they disagree. I apologise for any such moments – the victims can hold me entirely responsible.

In the passages which describe restoration, an extremely exacting, considered and methodical science, I have outlined the procedures in a slightly speeded up form for the sake of readability. The restorers whose work I have particularly featured – Simon Gillespie and Patrick Corbett – are extremely cautious professionals who may well balk at my untechnical descriptions and necessarily condensed accounts. In the process, I may also have unwittingly encouraged others less experienced to try restoration themselves. It is essential they do not. More damage has been done to pictures by amateur restorers than by any number of earthquakes or fires.

I have also been unable to do full justice to the academics, who tend to feature in these pages as edited bit-parts in the dramas of others, and without proper acknowledgement of the years of grind and scholarship that have won them their status as arbiters of authenticity. The countless art-history books on my shelves bear witness to their achievement, and many of the discoveries described in the following pages have only been made possible by their stamp of authority.

CHAPTER ONE

Cleaning-Off

ACETONE BIT THROUGH the brown varnish. From behind the restorer's shoulder, I could now see a bright mark on the subject's neck, contrasting sharply with the layer of grime across the rest of the picture, and growing ever larger with each dab of solvent. That's more like it, I thought, and looked forward to watching a hidden painting's dramatic return.

'There's something wrong,' he said. 'The varnish has moved too easily.' Agitated, the restorer poured more diluting spirit into the mixing jar, changed the swab, and began afresh. Again the varnish lifted instantly, increasing the size of hole into a wound, and causing him to pull away sharply. 'That's as far as I go,' he said, removing his magnifying lenses and handing them to me for a look. I tightened them to my head, changed places, peered into the test, and felt instant and sick regret. Instead of well-preserved 18th-century paint, there were no more than scant remains, indicating that the portrait was a ghostly remnant of its former self. What, ten minutes earlier, I thought might have been the opening chapter in the discovery of an opaquely dirty Gainsborough, had become the first stage in uncovering a worthless wreck of scrubbed canvas bereft of much of its original paint. The 'dirty' varnish had obviously been added in the last six months to conceal its plight and lure a potential customer. Bugger, I thought, that customer is me. It was my first year as a dealer, and it taught me a lesson I have never forgotten.

For discovering pictures, it is of immeasurable help to understand condition. Not only is this skill critical in deciding upon value, but indispensable if one is to recognise the work of an artist which to other eyes is hidden from view. Some of the most thrilling revelations have been made by dealers who know enough about the physical condition of pictures, and an artist's technique, to be able to detect an authentic and well-preserved work beneath an obscuring layer of dirt or over-paint. But there is always an element of risk. The painting beneath, once uncovered, may be so badly damaged that it is of little commercial value, indeed quite probably worth less than the amount paid for it out of optimism (the above example was worth even less than that!). What looked like a great and subtle work of art through enhancing grime could, after cleaning, turn out to be a crude copy. Furthermore, some dirty outer layers are so impregnable to solvents that they can only be removed with radical techniques that risk damaging the picture beneath. But this is where the professional thrives, and his judgements and gambles are amongst the most heartstopping in the business.

It is hard luck on the auctioneers if a sleeper is found in this way, because with some pictures there is often no way of working out what they are except by cleaning. And yet only in exceptional cases do the auctioneers recommend restoration. This is partly because by tampering with a painting's surface they risk removing its mysterious allure – and as a rule dirty pictures in what are described as 'country-house condition' sell better than cleaned ones. Also, as most auctions contain a high percentage of pictures consigned by dealers, most dealers know that if they see something completely clean and restored there is a chance it has been hanging very recently in one of their competitors' galleries and has, for one reason or another, failed to sell. Restoring and cleaning is also expensive, and the auctioneer as agent, rather than principal, cannot always justify the cost. The vendor is often not that keen on the expense either. Furthermore, the cleaning process might also reveal a proverbial 'can of worms', and a picture that has suffered, however well patched up, will deter many potential buyers.

In the case of an interesting painting which is so hidden by over-paint and dirt that it cannot be properly assessed, cataloguing is often vague by necessity. The auction department may well be thrown off the scent altogether, and miss the artist's identity. Often, however, particularly with the more professional cataloguers, they will attribute it correctly to the artist whose work they suspect lies beneath but use words such as 'circle of' or 'school of' – nebulous terms which place a painting amongst the artist's contemporaries or followers, but avoid commitment to firm authentication. These pictures then carry estimates that reflect the auctioneer's uncertainty and are often a fraction of those for fully ascribed works. It is here, and in the case of attributions that are missed altogether, that the knowledgeable risk-taker can prosper.

* * *

I have placed these types of discoveries into two categories: those pictures that are obscured by the conventional dirt of time (which includes tobacco- and fire-smoke, pollution and oxidisation – *see Fig.1*, which shows a cross-section of a paint sample overlaid with dirt) and works that, for whatever reason, have been over-painted by later restorers and artists thereby not just obscuring, but sometimes wholly concealing part or all of the painting beneath. The latter are dealt with in the next chapter, but in many instances they straddle both categories. Dealers with the hard experience of buying, restoring and reselling have an unfair advantage over the auctioneers whose experience is in finding, cataloguing and selling the 'raw material'. They are less involved in what is described by one particular dealer in London as 're-presentation' – or, put another way, the entire process of re-habilitating a work of art from an obscured, underrated picture into a major piece of retail stock. That dealer's name is Richard Knight.

'The best place to look at auction catalogues is in the window-seat of an aeroplane,' says Richard. 'The light is so bright and pure that it shows the details incomparably.' This was the cir-cumstance of his first glimpse of lot 259 in a sale of old masters at Sotheby's New York, which was to take place in three days' time. He was on the morning flight from London with the catalogue open on his lap, looking down at a lot, illustrated in black and white, of a middle-aged Antwerp couple holding hands in front of a draped curtain and landscape. It was catalogued as 'Attributed to Van Dyck', but Sotheby's commercial assessment of the picture was indicated by the paltry estimate of $10,000–$15,000: as a real Van Dyck, in good condition, it might have been priced at well over ten times that amount. A line of prov-enance stated that the vendors were the Detroit Institute of Arts, and that the large oil painting ($47^{1}/_{4} \times 60^{5}/_{8}$ inches) was being sold to benefit future, presumably more worthwhile, acquisitions for the museum.

Richard runs Colnaghi, one of the oldest and best-established old-masters dealers in London, and was on his way to New York for a buying trip. His company aims to buy and sell the best-quality early-European works the market offers, particularly Italian, and in its two-hundred-year history has helped line the walls of many of the world's leading art galleries and museums. Richard joined the firm in 1984, having run his own dealing and restoring practice, but began his art career fifteen years earlier in 1969, when he decided to turn down a university place in favour of a cataloguing job at Phillips the auctioneers in London

— a stable that has produced many of today's leading British art and antique dealers. He also enjoyed drawing and was fascinated with restoration and its capacity to revive and 're-present' the underrated. He spent many hours at the elbow of London restorers, observing how skilful cleaning and conservation could bring back pictures from the dead, how expert retouching to areas of paint loss could redefine shapes and tones which the original artist had intended, but that had been all but lost with the assaults of time. As a trader on his own, Richard's practical and intellectual skills combined to make a potent combination, and other dealers knew it. So did Colnaghi, and after the second of two invitations he finally agreed to join forces with them in 1984. He was then 33 and felt he had gained enough experience for the responsibility. Five years ago, on the departure of Richard Herner, the man who had finally persuaded him to join the company, he took over as joint managing director; and in early January 1993 he proved, in a startlingly public way, just how powerful his broad discipline can be.

With the benefit of the ethereal light that streamed through the aeroplane's porthole window that morning, Richard was growing excited. He could also see why the cataloguers had been so dismissive. He remembers thinking that the problems centred critically on the female figure's face. Judging by the black-and-white illustration, she had dark shadows to the rims of her eyes that gave her a hard and murderous look, so far away from the grace and finesse of Van Dyck as to make an attribution to the master seem implausible (*see Fig. 2*). Unperturbed by this, however, he was already formulating an excuse. 'Looking at the face of the lady compared with other elements in the picture,' he recalls, 'I couldn't help feeling that there was something unnecessary, a residue of dirty varnish in fact, that had built up round her eyes.' This was now Richard Knight the restorer talking. Whereas some dealers might have realised that there was a condition problem with her eyes, Richard had taken it further.

'You have to imagine,' he said, 'a judicious restorer attempting to clean a Van Dyck without damaging it in the process.' Solvents that remove varnish, and thereby clean a dirty picture, can sometimes also take away layers of original paint beneath – particularly 'glaze' or paint that has been mixed liberally with oil or varnish for the subtle finishing touches. For a restorer, cleaning these areas would have therefore been a perilous task, and Richard knew the problem from experience: 'When he came to the eyes and sockets, where Van Dyck's paint is notoriously vulnerable, he might well have held up, choosing to avoid the risk of cleaning off original paint beneath the dirty varnish.'

The result was before him. The lady's eyes, with their accumulation of dirty varnish, stood out chillingly in an otherwise light surround. She had taken on the appearance of a ghoul – albeit one in a well-preserved state. Remove that discoloured varnish, Richard suspected, and from beneath could emerge a genuine and sensitive work, worthy of the master himself.

Richard had had previous experience of the period of Van Dyck on which he was basing his assumptions. Going by subject and style, he knew that the picture had to by Van Dyck during his period in Antwerp, when he was around twenty years old, and closely associated with his master, Rubens. Some years earlier Richard had closely examined a Van Dyck portrait of the same period which had been cleaned by the master restorer John Brealey, and had become intimately acquainted with the precocious young artist's techniques. He had been able carefully to study the way Van Dyck had moved his brush, mixed the colour and applied thin layers of diluted pigment to the more subtle areas. Now he brought the memory of this experience into play; but to conclusively prove his hunches, he needed to see the painting 'in the flesh'.

On touching down in New York, he took a yellow cab straight to Sotheby's, a modern box-shaped building at the end of a block near Manhattan's Riverside. Fired by his memory of the illustration, he checked in his coat and cases and, freed of his baggage, went looking for the painting on the first-floor auction area – an expansive three-roomed arrangement, with the scale and proportions of a department store, and over three hundred pictures lining the walls and partitions, watched over by hovering security guards and porters in green overalls.

As he made his way slowly across the room, greeting other New York and London dealers and assessing the pictures, it became a matter of concern that this large canvas, the size of a small door on its side, was not on display. It should have been extremely conspicuous. By the time he had reached the third room, the unthinkable occurred to him. The picture had been withdrawn: the auctioneers had realised an error, and had decided to re-catalogue it for the next sale with a firm attribution. This gruesome inevitability started to take root, and just as he was accustoming himself to the acute disappointment, he glimpsed the edge of a large gilt frame, not hanging in the room, but in a corridor leading off it. As he approached, so his spirits began to lift. Placed in an obscure passageway, alone and almost over-looked, were the 17th-century couple from Detroit.

The final and critical verdict would be decided upon now. But Richard is a consummate dealer, and when presented with a discovery of his own making, his commercial faculties work in tandem with his emotions. His reaction was typically pragmatic. 'In that one glance, in the split second I was able to see it, I knew it was to be bought. I could see it was by Van Dyck and that its condition – though superficially off-putting – was extremely fine. But,' he added, and here he was emphatic, 'there is of course a limit to what such a thing is worth. To buy a discovery, whatever the price, just because you have discovered it, is a form of vanity which can quickly lead to bankruptcy.' He conceded, however, that this represented a 'first-rate commercial opportunity', and that within professional bounds he continued to be highly excited.

The picture was exactly as he had forecast. In the relative privacy of the corridor he looked closely at the lady's eyes and observed the build-up of congealed dirty varnish – it conformed precisely to his theory of partial cleaning leading to cosmetic imbalance. He looked closely at the brush work across the rest of the picture and observed the familiar strokes of the young artist, and his trait of using paint without oil, giving the pigment the consistency of dried paste. He also noted the abbreviated way the landscape was painted – 'at a hell of a lick' – which he had also observed in the other early Van Dyck that had been cleaned by Brealey. The only possible discrepancy was an overall layer of blue-grey dirt that gave the picture an even more mournful appearance and which had not been visible from the photograph. This, combined with the earlier dirt that lay in the brushed grooves of the 'impasto' or thicker areas of paint, and which earlier restorers had been unable to reach with cleaning agents, particularly around the hands, further inhibited its qualities and fully explained why both the museum and auction house had been so dismissive.

That night Richard discussed the picture with Nicholas Hall, the urbane young English President of Colnaghi, New York, who had arrived from London five years earlier. He fully agreed with Richard that this was the only picture they wanted in the sale, and duly arranged for one of his anonymous agents to execute the bid. As Colnaghi's is known for its expertise, there was no point attracting unnecessary attention to the picture by bidding in person. Together they therefore settled upon a figure up to which they felt happy to entrust the agent. They both agreed that if the picture cleaned as they hoped, it would re-present a substantial work of the 'middle range' by Van Dyck – not a major masterpiece, but a significant early work, probably from his first Antwerp period, and worth up to half a million pounds. They weren't going to 'go mad', and would do their best to secure it for a price well beneath that. If they were successful in their bidding, the picture could be cleaned in time to include it in their next major New York exhibition of old masters in the spring.

Nicholas and Richard stood at the back of the saleroom, their agent, a local New York dealer, sat five rows from the front. The picture was buried deep into the afternoon's business, and as this was Sotheby's less important old-master sale (they had a major one coming up later that season) and it was now the afternoon session of lesser works, there was a correspondingly small turnout. About fifty prospective buyers had pitched up, either sitting in the seats provided, lining the walls, or gathered nonchalantly at the back holding open their catalogues and chatting to colleagues. I can remember the event well because I was there also, and following the picture's fortune. As I recall, the bidding started at around $6,000, in other words $4,000 beneath the painting's lower estimate. The Colnaghi buyer got his hand up early at $9,000 and, for a short while – about five or six seconds – it seemed that he was about to buy it against the auctioneer's reserve, which is normally 10 per cent beneath the lower estimate. But, having waited for his moment, Larry Steigrad, a young New York old-master dealer then newly established, took up the bidding from the left of the room. With tremendous speed the price soared to around $70,000, and then Larry dropped out. The auctioneer checked his pace and looked around the room for more offerings.

A tall figure in a Loden coat, standing at the back, then took up the challenge. It was the instantly recognizable presence of Richard Herner, none other than the ex-managing director of Colnaghi's, now working on his own and bidding against Richard Knight – the man he had recruited eleven years ago. But any irony would have been lost to both Herner and the rest of the room at the time: only Richard Knight and Nicholas Hall knew that the tenacious seated bidder was the agent of Colnaghi. At $125,000 Richard Herner dropped out, and his ex-protégé bought the picture, together with buyer's premium, for the equivalent of £75,000. It had been expensive – but substantially within their planned purchase price.

* * *

Richard wet a small sponge under the tap, wrung out the excess water and, together with Nicholas, surveyed the picture in front of them. They had managed to clear it from Sotheby's and have it delivered to their gallery on 59th Street by 7pm that evening, and it now lay against the showroom wall, its mute, discoloured surface lit by the overhead gallery lights. This was the bit Richard loved – the practical fusing with the intellectual, the central moment in the evolution of re-presentation when the picture's visual potential is first revealed. Sometimes, but not always, superficial dirt such as mild smoke-staining and everyday air-borne pollutants can be removed by water, much like washing skin; soap can also increase the effectiveness of the process and even plain spit contains a useful cleaning agent. They are insufficient for removing ingrained or hardened dirt, but even these extremely mild solvents will sometimes produce startling results.

Richard slowly dragged the sponge across the sky, the area they had decided to explore first. The immediate effect was similar to that seen in corny advertisements for household cleaners: the damp yellow sponge turned dark brown, the top layer of the picture's surface lifted, and in the sponge's wake came a bright, blue-white trail. Although the paint revealed was still stained, the washed area of sky shone out vibrantly, in contrast to the untouched areas all around, indicating the enormous change to the picture even a superficial clean would bring about.

They later gave the painting to a professional restorer in London who was able to clean off all the layers of dirty varnish, including the accumulation around the lady's face, and that ingrained in the paint grooves (*Fig. 3*). He revealed a work in near-perfect condition. Although the lady's eyes were still dark, in removing the discoloured varnish they became crucially lighter, and her macabre stare softened into seductive self-assurance – she assumed one of the arresting expressions of early 17th-century nobility which Van Dyck seems to have both defined and created. Apart from some minor areas of localised loss where the picture had been dented or scratched, such as on the tip of the man's nose, it proved to be a painting in an unusually well-preserved state, particularly for an early example of the artist's work. In the summer of that year Colnaghi sold it to the Museum of South Australia for $1 million (Australian dollars), about £450,000, as a fully authenticated and welcome re-addition to Van Dyck's recorded body of early works.

* * *

To watch your painting reborn through cleaning is, for me, far and away the high point of the business. I have spent hours that would add up to months doing nothing other than looking over my long-suffering restorer's shoulder, as solvents, scalpels and consummate technical skill attempt to salvage hidden works. It normally happens after work when all the staff have gone home, the telephone and other impositions of the day have ceased, and he can operate undisturbed, applying himself with the intense concentration that the perilous task requires. It can hold you in a state of terrified enchantment to see the brushstrokes on your recently bought picture newly revealed after a hundred years of hiding as, layer by layer, centimetre by centimetre, the under-lying work is laid bare. I know of nothing that makes time travel faster, hours pass in minutes like speeded-up film; and I dread the moment when the restorer decides to pack up for the day (or, in one particular case, when his wife rings up to summon him home), and the picture's fate is still undecided. For it can end distressingly too. Sometimes, as happened with my 'Gains-borough' at the beginning of the chapter, beneath the dirt and over-paint a sickly and unsaleable painting is revealed, too worn or damaged to be rescued.

One of the first pictures that I bought in America was revealed by the skill of the restorer. Getting on for six years ago, I received from a major New York auction house a catalogue for one of their regular old-master sales. It included British portraits as well – my area of specialisation – and, flipping through the pages, I noticed a black-and-white illustration of a head-and-shoulders portrait described as 'John Julius Angerstein' and attributed to the 'Circle of Sir Thomas Lawrence' (*Fig. 4*), with an estimate of $3,000–$4,000 (£2,000–£2,600 approximately). Lawrence (1769–1830) was the leading portrait painter of his day, a boy genius who practised as a professional portrait painter in pastels when a young teenager in Bath, and went on to become the most sought-after face painter in Regency England. His works hang in major museums and art galleries throughout the world, and good ones are avidly bought by collectors whenever they emerge on the market. The term 'circle of' as used in the catalogue, indicated that the auction house did not regard it as a genuine work by Lawrence, but that in their opinion it was executed by another artist at the same period, and showing the master's influence. Angerstein was a highly successful businessman of Russian extraction, working and living in London at the end of the 18th and early 19th centuries and, together with Lawrence, formed a collection of pictures which provided the core of the National Gallery collection. Lawrence's celebrated full-scale portrait of him now hangs in the library of Lloyd's of London, and, locating an illustration of that picture, I placed it beside the painting in the auction catalogue to compare the two images (*Fig. 5*). Although distinctly inferior in comparison, the head in the catalogue was clearly related to the famous image. The features were practically identical and the face was posed at the same angle. But the picture in the auction had distinct shortcomings: the features were less well-defined, and what were brilliantly slick strokes in the Lloyd's Angerstein looked congealed and pasty here, giving it the immediate appearance of a copy.

Above the catalogue entry it stated that this was the property of an American museum who were selling it, together with a number of other pictures, as Detroit had done with their Van Dyck, in order to raise funds. This apparently crude copy, I surmised, had been deemed of insufficient quality for public exhibit and therefore deaccessioned without regret. But despite the painting's comparatively rough appearance, on looking at it further it was alleviated by one aspect: it had a look to the eyes which, if taken in isolation, was sharp and arresting, and beckoned closer enquiry. Being your average dealer, I therefore complied, and made arrangements to view this, and other pictures, the following week in America.

The morning flight to New York arrived in good time for me to be able to view Christie's that afternoon. Amongst the numerous Italian and Dutch old masters I found the picture hanging in their upstairs gallery, at the end of a line of mediocre British paintings, and on looking deeply into its discoloured surface, the first thing I noticed was that there was more in the picture than I had seen from the photograph. For the first time, I could make out perfunctory strokes around Angerstein's lapels, which I had not properly understood from the illustration, and which added a sketched suggestion of a coat. Irritatingly, however, the paint around the head and in the blocked-in area of his coat was so dirty that I could barely assess how it related to its background. Furthermore, the face was so disfigured by ingrained dirt that it had the effect of flattening the contours of his features, particularly on the left-hand side, making a judgement of the painting's quality almost impossible. I was therefore obliged to do what a number of art dealers are inclined to resort to in such situations: wetting my finger with saliva, I rubbed Mr Angerstein's left eye. This is a rather disgusting, but on occasion essential practice when dealing with dirty pictures, for the effect of saliva on dirty matt varnish is rather like that of white spirit or turpentine, in that it creates a glossy 'lens' through which you can see more clearly the paint beneath. It also gives you the opportunity to visualise, in a small area at least, what the painting may look like when cleaned. This may seem rather shocking to a generation used to treating art with due reverence. Certainly, if you tried it on a picture hanging in a national museum, you would probably be lynched by the security staff. An extremely discoloured picture up for sale, however, so obscured by dirty varnish that normal eyesight is unable to detect what lies beneath, is an entirely different matter. Although not actively encouraged by the auction houses, for works of lesser stature they will turn a blind eye to a potential buyer who needs to obtain more information about a picture's hidden depths (or lack of them) before parting with any money. The same ends can be achieved by subjecting the picture to fierce light, or a dab of white spirit which later evaporates off, but this is not always possible to arrange, and these more elaborate exercises – which often involve conspicuously removing the picture from the room – can unnecessarily alert both the auction staff and other buyers. Spittle does have a down-side, however. It leaves a cloudy smear. This is easily removed after the sale, but an interesting and dirty picture may have had the spit test done to it many times at the preview, particularly around the signature. By the time it comes under the hammer its surface can look as blemished as a hand-streaked car windscreen. Private vendors, who occasionally attend sales to bid their pictures farewell, have been known, on seeing their heirloom shockingly obscured by smears, to cry out in dismay. They should, in fact, feel cheered: the trade has been showing close interest.

The temporary effect of the spittle test was striking. The blue tones resonated and the strongly applied white highlights sparkled. Just above the eye, strands of different colours also became visible, giving more depth and variety to the upper contours of the face. Doing the same test on the other eye, I was then momentarily transfixed by the combination of both. With stern intensity, they bored out of the discoloured surround.

The sale was two days later. On the morning, I arrived early, and for a consideration asked one of the porters if he could fetch the painting from the stacks to give me the opportunity of a last look. By this time a few other people had already gone through the same exploration process as I had, and Angerstein's visage was streaked and clouded. But my second look at the work confirmed the first: something wonderful lay beneath this discoloured surface and, provided the picture remained within affordable bounds, I would try and find out what it was.

The sale was well attended with a large swathe of Italian dealers draped against the back walls, hoovering-up any well-priced Italian old masters. The main English dealers were also present, as were many members of the American trade. I did not expect much competition – an odd-looking English portrait like this is not the sort of picture that attracts mainstream old-master dealers – but I prepared myself for a bid of $10,000 in case one of the other 'smearers' had developed a hunch. The picture came up, I lifted my hand, but despite some strenuous pleas from the auctioneer there was only one other bid, from the telephone, against which I bought it for $5,500 – approximately £4,000 with buyer's premium of ten per cent.

Having picked it up from the auction room that afternoon, I walked back to my hotel room at the Westbury on 69th and Madison, and propped the painting against a chair at the end of my bed. Taking the shade off my bedside light in order to make the beam more intense, and now freed from the observations of anyone around me, I then intimately examined the grime-covered surface. By this time I had taken it out of its frame, managing to lever back the nails with the help of a coin, and had a clear view of the canvas edges. The original canvas had been laid on to a newer one. The placing of an old canvas on to new is a very common occurrence with paintings over a hundred years old and is know as 're-lining'. Canvas, a biodegradable material, is subject to deterioration, particularly in a damp environment, and restorers often recommend that old pictures be re-supported in this way to help return them to their original appearance. Done badly, it can crush the pigment of a picture, and has been the cause of countless wrecked old masters. In this case, however, the surface appeared relatively unscathed.

The original canvas was clearly old, at least 150 years, which would be consistent with something produced in the period of Sir Thomas Lawrence. Generally speaking, old English canvas is coarser, the wove more conspicuous than in later canvases, and this provides a useful pointer in the dating process. On my way back to the hotel room, I had also called at a drugstore and purchased a bottle of white spirit and a large bag of cotton wool. Pulling out a swab, I now applied the spirit to an area around Angerstein's head. White spirit works not altogether unlike spit in producing a temporary shiny surface on a matt one, allowing you to gaze through dirty varnish for as long as it remains either unabsorbed or unevaporated, and under the bright light I could begin to see revealing physical inconsistencies in the painted surface. The brown background, which shone like wet sludge, did not have the appearance of the contrastingly older paint in the face and where there was the suggestion of a coat. It showed neither signs of cracking – a sure symptom of age – nor the same thick build-up of layers, and therefore had all the evidence of having been applied later. It then occurred to me, for the first time, that we could be dealing with a genuine head-sketch.

When Lawrence died there were about 150 unfinished paintings left in his studio, many of them begun 20 or 30 years earlier and to which he had not returned. He was not a natural businessman, became rather disorganised in later life, and often let his clients down – starting commissions which he was then unable to finish. He also kept sketches in his studio so that he could produce replicas, particularly in the case of famous or popular sitters, for which there was always a demand. Without having to gain another sitting, and working from the head-sketch, Lawrence could either produce the painting himself, or farm it out to one of his assistants. Many remain in existence today and it now appeared that this could be a head-sketch of Angerstein, one of his most distinguished clients and friends. As Angerstein was a notable figure in his day, there would have been a number of likely clients for portraits of the great benefactor and patron, particularly as the primary image, the one in Lloyd's, was a much celebrated portrait in its time. Equally this could be a another portrait of Angerstein that had been begun by Lawrence but not finished. In any event, to know more, I now had to have the painting cleaned and restored.

I arrived at Heathrow airport at about 8am and later that morning rang my restorer, Simon Gillespie, to ask him whether I could bring in a new and exciting picture later that day. The fervour of a possible discovery had the effect of banishing jet lag, and when I entered his studio after work that evening, I found myself distinctly alert.

I had first met Simon seven or eight years earlier when he was working from a converted drawing room in a house in Brixton, and I remember thinking that if you were playing a parlour game trying to match people's appearances to their professions, his would floor you. He is a squarely built, red-haired, moustached Celt who is known to shin up mountains in his spare time, and his physique looks adapted for the job. But when it comes to critical restoration he works with the virtuosity of a master watch-maker. He relishes the complex problems, and is at his best when painstakingly removing layers of added paint, an often terrifyingly exacting and stressful task, particularly when the pigment beneath is easily dissolvable and therefore fugitive. In the case of many English portraits, more often than not it is.

Simon took the painting from me and placed it on his easel.

The lights of the restorer are rather like those of an operating theatre, and are particularly crucial in the first stage of a picture's assessment. He directed their beams directly upon the new arrival, and for fifteen minutes we did nothing but observe, speculating on what could be original paint, and what was blackened varnish, all the time referring to an illustration of the Lloyd's picture for comparison. In those days he was working upstairs in a warehouse near London Bridge, and the square, breeze-blocked room had the feeling of a laboratory. Microscopes, lenses and numerous bottles of labelled chemicals lined the shelves, and when on the scent of discovery, I had seen him bring them into play with the adeptness and passion of a great alchemist.

Simon took down a bottle of acetone, poured a small amount into a mixing dish, and added a liberal measure of diluting white spirit. Selecting one from a bunch of thin wooden sticks, he then scored the end with a penknife and pushed it into a pile of cotton wool, twisting it as he did so, to create a home-made cotton wool bud with which to apply the solution. He reached for his pair of magnifying lenses, locked them on to his head, and rolled up his sleeves. Now ready and positioned upon a stool in front of the picture, he turned to me for confirmation. 'This is the point of no return. Once we start taking this off we'll never be able to put it back again, you know.' This is, of course, always the case with a would-be discovery in need of restoration. If it turned out to be unsalvageable, we would be left with a conspicuously damaged picture, showing all the signs of failed restoration, and therefore a less saleable item than that with which we started: it had already happened to me a number of times before. By now, however, I was utterly committed, and going for all or bust. The picture was of little use to anyone in its present state, I reflected, and least of all an art dealer who has just bought it with barely a single hand raised in competition by his discerning colleagues.

Paint and varnish react to solvents according to their varying constituents, and the length of time they have been allowed to dry. Part of the art and science of a restorer, for which he is often assiduously trained at college and then afterwards in apprenticeship, is to find the critical chemical balance which will remove the dirty varnish and any added layers of paint, but which is not so strong that it will 'burn' through into the original layer beneath. Observing this essential discipline of approach, Simon therefore started with a very dilute mixture of acetone to white spirit in order to establish the minimum strength required for removal of the top layer of dirty varnish.

He dipped the bud into the liquid and, with a rolling action, gently applied it to the top right-hand corner of the canvas. Seconds later, he wiped the test area down with a large hand-held swab soaked in white spirit, and examined it for signs of any removed dirt. Nothing had happened so he tried again, this time giving the solvent longer to act. Still the varnish layer remained impermeable. 'We need to go stronger,' he said, and poured more acetone into the solution to increase its bite. This time it worked. The cotton-wool bud perforated the layer of varnish, turning the wool a muddy yellow, and Simon rapidly sponged the square centimetre area clean to reveal a shallow indentation of darker brown. He passed me his lenses and I was allowed to peer into the aperture. It took a moment or two to focus, but with another helping dab of white spirit I began to make out, within the indentation, an area of smooth, unbroken paint. This had nothing in common with the texture of Angerstein's face, which had 'craquelure'. As a rule, old paint shows its age in this way: webs of cracks, or *craquelure*, testify to the length of time old pigments have been allowed to dry and naturally degrade, and they often contrast tellingly with later, added layers, which are unbroken. The implication was that we had further to go to reach the original layer. Simon changed his bud, dipped it in the solvent, and then reapplied it to the same area. This time the bud became thickly saturated with a mixture of later paint and dirty varnish. Swabbing the area clean, from within the test area there now appeared a startling patch of orange-brown. For a horrible moment I thought we had burnt through to the raw canvas beneath. 'What on earth's that?' I asked. 'It's what's beneath,' Simon replied smartly, replacing another bud that had become impossibly congealed and tacky.

Scraping away at the thick surface, over the next hour he proceeded to expose a larger area of this scorching brown which grew in size to reveal a vibrant background of vibrant sandy-brown – a pristine layer of original paint, prepared by the artist as a surface on which to build up the picture. In other words, we were revealing primed canvas – the outer areas of an unfinished picture. The solvent, though strong enough to remove over-paint, left this layer of earlier, harder paint unscathed. Observing the emergence of such a pure and honest colour from beneath its later muddied crust was little short of miraculous, particularly as Simon approached the head and revealed a new colour – bottle-green – which had the effect of thrusting Angerstein's head forward, and almost out of the picture.

He then turned his attentions to the hair. Some of the same opaque varnish in the background was covering the top and side of Angerstein's head and, unaware how this area would react, he now changed to a more dilute solvent. He began on the left-hand side and the first thing to be uncovered was a springing, horn-like curl (*Fig.* 6), which had been blanketed out by the same muddy over-paint, and with this new addition the balance of the face altered substantially and moved perceptibly closer to the painting at Lloyd's.

The flesh was the easiest part of all. With each application of solvent, dirt lifted to reveal shining skin tones, bringing with it previously unseen contours to the cheeks and features. After an hour the face almost entirely revived, and a sparkling visage, framed in green, now stood out with near neon intensity against a rich brown background, the bright white of the hair, and the fleshy pink of the face giving it the clarity of a recently peeled shrimp. A dark splash of burgundy suggested Angerstein's coat, his eyes drilled the viewer with acid blue, and minute dribbles of white highlight made them glisten (*Fig. 7*).

Simon took off his lenses and asked if he could now go home. Like me, he was both elated and exhausted, but he had better reason to be. He had just raised from the dead an outstanding Lawrence sketch, bringing it back to the world in its vivid original form. Lawrence was a flashy and dazzling painter, and this was now as close as possible to the object he had left unfinished on his easel in the early years of the 19th century. Sometimes, 20th-century sensibilities are over-influenced by quaint concepts of antiquarianism, and therefore unsettled by works of this age or earlier which shine so brightly. But in their original setting, which in many instances was dark and candlelit, they were often intended as shimmering enhancements of their mundanely mortal subjects. There is a massive critical difference between a properly cleaned Regency portrait such as this, with all its original glazes intact, and one that has been harshly over-cleaned. If these final, filtering layers of modelling and subtle characterisation have been removed, the face can take on the appearance of a corpse. The one before us, however, with everything still in place, had the impact of a work just chanced upon in Lawrence's studio. It had the immediacy of something splashed upon the canvas the previous evening, and to which the master might soon return.

So why had the sketch ended up as it had? The answer is not dissimilar to what had happened Richard Knight's Van Dyck, but more speculative. The painting had become dirty and discoloured, as does all oil paint. Whoever attended to it first partly cleaned the face, and then may have turned to the background. Cleaning off a small area of varnish, the restorer may have been shocked, as I was at first, to find bright primer protruding through. What I suspect he then did was to cover this dirty background varnish with a veil of later paint, instead of cleaning it, thereby creating a disingenuous but solid appearance. He did not clean the lower half at all, nor add to it, and this discoloured primer contrasted with the dark pigment of the background to give the ghostly form of an upper body. But the combination of ineptly cleaned flesh and stolid surround rendered its appearance so untypical of genuine Lawrence that its true author was disguised.

Later that month I wrote to Kenneth Garlick, the acknowledged expert on Lawrence's work, asking him to come and view it in all its unclothed glory. I was somewhat taken aback when he replied that he had already given an opinion on the portrait, many years before, and had deemed it a copy. But he said he would be happy to come and see it again. To be fair, there was literally no way that either he, the museum who sold it, or the auction cataloguer could have confidently detected what lay beneath the surface of the painting in its disfigured state, and it was my particularly good fortune to have the services of an outstanding restorer to realise a hunch.

When he saw the portrait, Kenneth Garlick proclaimed it to be a high-quality and hitherto unknown sketch for the Lloyd's picture, and welcomed its emergence. It has since been acquired by a British collector.

CHAPTER TWO

Over-Paint

IF YOU WERE plunged into darkness in the National Gallery one night, and given an ultraviolet lamp to find your way, you would see the over-paint on some pictures with startling clarity. On the surfaces of Martyrdoms, Goya portraits and Dutch landscapes, fluorescing dots, blobs and specks would show up starkly against their background, looking like acts of indiscriminate vandalism.

But what you would actually be seeing is the opposite of vandalism. These are the signs of the painstaking 'retouchings' and 'filling-ins' of restorers who have expertly matched the colours and helped re-create forms in areas where paint has been lost or damaged. When an ultraviolet lamp is shined on the surface of a restored picture, the different materials in the painting such as the varnishes, paint media and retouchings transform the invisible ultraviolet light into visible frequencies (*Fig.* 8).

Paintings on display in the National Gallery are for the most part in fine condition, but almost without exception all pictures of age have suffered battering and assaults, either accidentally or by design, and the extremely fragile nature of paint on panel or canvas means that they bear their scars cruelly. The paint itself, or its support of canvas or panel, may have expanded and contracted in changing environments with resultant loss. The surface of the painting may have come into contact with a careless elbow or door handle when being moved. Before increased awareness and advances in modern restoration, over-cleaning was an all too common occurrence, and in the hands of amateur restorers still happens today. The cleaning solvent is a terribly dangerous blessing, and if allowed to dissolve through the top layers of varnish and over-paint into the genuine pigment beneath, the inept restorer can whip off original strokes. In the more sensitive areas of a picture this can happen without a moment's warning. But I have also seen portraits of Charles I with 17th-century sabre cuts and unprepossessing-looking ancestral portraits that have been used for air-rifle practice. For a painting over two hundred years old to show no sign of abuse or degradation – either by accident, environment or, less commonly, design – is virtually unheard of.

This leads to essential repair work, and is not to be confused with the main subject of this chapter, which is when the repair develops into improvement or change. The analogy of a plastic surgeon is appropriate here. To mend or disguise disfiguring scars is one definable aspect of a plastic surgeon's job. To consciously 'improve' a natural face means entering the realm of cosmeticism, which calls on a very different set of ethical and surgical considerations. Sometimes, however, the two will overlap. There is an argument that even repair work to a picture is unethical, and that the damaged object should be left in all its honest glory, with the disfiguring evidence of its history manifest. The majority of Western museums, however, do not take this more archaeological approach to their later panels and canvases, and instead try, with the aid of restoration, to return them as closely as possible to their original appearance, if damaged. Indeed, a gallery of paintings in their raw and untouched state would make a grim line-up to the casual visitor – the holes, scars, scratches and losses presenting a gruesome aesthetic distraction to the technically minded.

Sometimes repair work can be used to disguise frighteningly large areas of damage, and it's here that we begin to move into the more dramatic consequences of over-paint. This is a constant worry to the art dealer when assessing a repaired work, particularly when it comes to parting with money, and should be borne in mind as a disturbing risk underlying many of the stories in this book. I once bought a portrait of the 16th–17th-century playwright, Ben Jonson, from an auction in Greenwich, knowing that the hair had been over-painted, but hoping that it was mostly superficial and that beneath would be damaged, but salvageable original paint (over-paint is often applied excessively). I was to be proved horribly wrong. Before my eyes, as the solvents worked to remove the added 20th-century paint, I began to see a growing area of raw canvas beneath. By the end of the operation the dramatist had only half a head: the face stopped above the forehead, for in that area he had been over-cleaned at an earlier date, not just partially, but totally, leaving him semi-decapitated, like a nicely served boiled egg. This is always a risk when removing later paint from an old picture, but there is also such a thing as non-essential over-paint, which has little or nothing to do with repair, and is more accurately described as 're-painting'.

The reverence we show for works of art today is partly linked to their enormous value. The price for original art by esteemed artists has increased at such a disproportionate rate to so many other commodities that it has achieved a status similar to sacred relics, guarded and preserved and only to be tampered with in cases of absolute necessity. But this was not always the case, and the discoveries dealt with in this chapter are those that have been superficially disfigured at some point in their history either by design, out of ignorance, or both, and which are then dramatically returned to their former guise by 20th-century know-ledge and technology. These pictures have not had later paint added to repair them, but to change their appearance altogether.

One would now no sooner crayon over a Holbein drawing as put it into a paper shredder, but that is effectively what happened, in previous centuries, to a number of those in the Royal Collection at Windsor. The idea of changing aspects of an old master to satisfy middle-class prudery would be seen as barbarism today, but in the 19th century the National Gallery had a restorer who was known to paint out the 'private parts' of their more 'explicit' works, and in one instance went so far as to alter a wet-looking kiss into a dry one, in Bronzino's 'Allegory of Venus'. Museum directors, dealers, artists and connoisseurs held a different, less tolerant and more judgemental view of their paintings, and as the academic subject of art history was then comparatively hit-and-miss anyway, few purists were around to rebuke them.

As a result of this once prevailing attitude countless works of art have been doctored, only to pass down the generations and emerge in today's market. Faces that have been prettified, sketches 'completed' by another hand, religious pictures made less pious, and landscapes with added figures are all common occurrences. And it didn't only happen in centuries past. In the 1960s and '70s a strong dollar brought many American collectors to London who often preferred their pictures without blemishes – however old the works might be – and, skies and seas were sometimes obligingly painted over by dealers to disguise the natural cracking or *craquelure* in the paint. Sometimes customers would insist on alterations. One colleague recalls, a number of years ago, being told by a Middle Eastern client that an 18th-century horse picture could only be considered for his collection if its tail was docked – so that it looked like his living present-day racehorses! The implicit request was firmly declined.

When major adaptations are made, the style of the original

painter, the all-important hallmarks of an artist's character that determine attribution, are often so obscured by change and addition that they are sometimes no longer regarded as authentic. Scholarship has progressed dramatically, and for every major artist there is now a reference library of illustrations and photographs; by quick comparison to these, 'enhanced' works can look quite implausible. Ironically, therefore, advances in modern art history can mean that these otherwise genuine works are dismissed as crude copies or pastiches. The perspicacious buyer, combining their own talents with those of a brilliant restorer, can then sometimes revive these pictures with glorious results.

The tendency for meddling painters to 'finish off' what an earlier artist began has given rise to a number of these discoveries in recent years, and a memorable example was uncovered in 1992 by the Bond Street art consultant and dealer Deborah Gage. Debo, as she is known, was born in Zambia and came to England when she was thirteen years old when 'art', she recalls, 'hit me with an enormous passion.' This happened partly as a result of her propitious early contact with wonderful examples of art at the Gage family's ancestral home, Firle Place, in Sussex. Her regard for great art and antiques is matched by her love of nature and the African bush, and it would be fair to describe her approach to the subject of dealing as intuitive and innate: she regrets the odd occasions when her intellectual faculties have overridden the instinctual or 'gut' feelings upon which many of her art-historical judgements rest. This form of intelligence is ideal when it comes to seeing 'through' pictures which have been obscured or disguised, when the field of vision has become so clogged with over-paint that normal critical assessment is impossible.

Debo first saw the landscape when it was produced from a cupboard in the home of an American client, whom she was visiting during her constant round-the-world travels. To look at initially it was a pretty sorry sight (*Fig. 9*). A blobby, dirty landscape of a cottage and pond, approximately one foot high and one and a half across, to an art dealer's eye it had more the appearance of a late-Victorian amateur daub than a work by John Constable, the originally hoped-for artist. Her client had bought the picture for £250 from Sotheby's just under twenty years earlier, in 1974, when it had been catalogued as by 'J. Constable' – the use of the initial rather than the full first name being an old-fashioned way for the auction room to indicate doubtful authenticity. At the time of purchase it could have been seen as a high price to pay for a work of apparently rather poor quality and, slightly regretting it, Debo's client had thereafter consigned it to a cupboard.

Debo's first reaction as she angled the painting into the light was fairly dismissive. She had seen countless uninteresting works by followers of Constable throughout her career and was used, more often than not, to rejecting them. But just as she was about to hand it back something attracted her attention. At first she couldn't place it, but as she allowed her gaze to dwell on the painting's surface she began to feel that there were some elements in the picture that were better than others: there were signs that the painter, whoever he may have been, had captured the landscape's mood and form. Trying to ignore the off-putting, cloddy strokes in the trees, she began to observe that some of the clouds were sketched in with a sureness and ease, and that the walls of the cottage resonated with the bold use of bright white pigment. In other words, amidst the mess of paint, there were convincing passages worthy of a good artist. But then her eye traversed the muddy, ill-defined stream and some of the bushes, which looked as though they had been shaped in putty. *This*, she thought, was surely too far away from the fluid characteristics of Britain's greatest landscape painter.

Staving off her doubts, she asked her client if they could take the painting out of its frame in order to view it more clearly.

This is an often essential act in the judgement of a picture. As was the case with the portrait of Angerstein in the previous chapter, removing the frame allows you to see the unpainted edge of the canvas, and thereby establish more about the ground on which the image is painted. It can also be tantamount to seeing a work 'without its clothes on' — as the artist would have executed the picture, and unenhanced by a frame.

Removing the nails and corks with pliers, she lifted the painting free, and examined the perimeter. Through the darkened varnish she was able to make out a small step — a line of paper finishing barely a millimetre from the edge of the canvas. This indicated that it was not in fact a work on canvas, but on paper, which had subsequently been laid down on a canvas support. It was now becoming exciting. Constable did not produce his sketches as finished works, but as *aides-mémoires* — hurried observations and ideas which he would sometimes throw down on pieces of paper and card, and then later use as the source for his formal and commissioned oil paintings. If only the painting had looked better, Debo had thought earlier, it could be one of these sketches. Now, out of its frame, and with the benefit of her continuing observations, it was beginning to look possible.

There was little more Debo could do there and then, so she asked her client whether he could send the picture to England. There, with the benefit of national art-historical expertise and restoration, it might be possible to take her hunches further. Her client, who had always harboured a hope that this picture might turn out to be better than it looked, happily agreed.

It was to Leslie Parris, the Tate Gallery's resident expert on Constable, that Debo took it next. Some years earlier he had helped assemble a major Tate exhibition of the artist's works, and Debo made an appointment to show it to him, as soon as it arrived. When first presented with the strange-looking landscape he reacted as Debo had done, with instant doubts, but the longer he looked at it, the more intrigued he became. He wanted first to address an inconsistency to do with the picture's size. In this respect his reaction was typically academic. His scholarship and knowledge had taught him to expect distinct traits which a dealer might not necessarily be aware of, and the picture's rather unusual dimensions, $13^5/_8 \times 17^1/_4$ inches (34.6×43.7 cm), were not typical of Constable (his landscape sketches are generally smaller). But he knew the subject related closely to a major work by Constable entitled 'Valley Farm' which depicted the cottage belonging to Constable's acquaintance, Willy Lot, a tenant farmer in Flatford Mill, Suffolk. Turning to an illustration of one of Constable's drawings for the composition, which he had close to hand in the exhibition catalogue, he then came up with the possible answer. The page of his sketchbook on which the pencil drawing for the painting had been executed had been extended with a glued-on addition, indicating that Constable was at pains to incorporate this unusually broad, picturesque scene in a way that was for him untypical. If this oil sketch were to be by Constable it might, therefore, explain why it was unusually large. This theorising, however, could only take them so far. Something had happened to this landscape, and if it were to emerge as an original work by the artist, it would have to be undone.

A man with possibly more experience of the physical properties of Constable's work than any other is the restorer John Bull. He has worked on numerous examples of the artist's works on paper and canvas, and has earned an incomparable reputation in the restoration world for his diligence and skill with rare and important pictures. It was to him, in his studio in Wimbledon, that Debo took the painting next. John Bull examined it carefully but, needing time to do a careful technical analysis, asked her to leave it with him. He then telephoned a few days later to say that he had done a test which had proved positive. Although he could not promise anything, it looked as though the over-paint might lift, and if Debo cared to return in a few weeks' time, more would be revealed.

Debo returned a month later, with Leslie Parris. Rounding the door into Bull's studio and setting eyes upon the picture from ten yards away, she recalls feeling knocked over by the impact. As she walked closer she realised that there was now no doubt. This was a genuine and sparkling Constable sketch (*Fig. 10*).

The composition was exactly the same. Its tonality and character, however, had been transformed. With the aid of solvents, the painting that had lain in a cupboard for the last twenty years had now been stripped of its daubs of green in the trees, and of the thick additions in the stream, to return it to a fluid, spontaneous outdoor sketch. Attempting to 'finish it', probably to make it more commercial, at some point during the last hundred years an 'artist' had decided to carry on where Constable had left off. He had filled in the more sketchy areas of the foliage, and entirely repainted the foreground water, clumsily blanketing the atmospheric, sketchy suggestions. It was never meant to be completed, but what the rogue artist had done was the equivalent of taking a landscape by, say, Monet and, thinking he could resolve his impressionistic forms, had taken out his paintbrush and tried to do so. No doubt the unknown painter had thought he was improving the Constable sketch, but the outcome had been an implausible daub. Thankfully, however, there were some areas – a large part of the sky and the side of the cottage – which he had felt unable to improve, and it was these passages of original paint that had communicated themselves to Debo. Thus what was once a grubby, contrived-looking amateur work had, with exacting restoration and the use of carefully balanced solvents, been returned to a brilliantly observed Constable sketch – the trees, sky and cottage caught as if in the blink of an eye. Leslie Parris unequivocally accepted it as a preparatory oil sketch for one of Constable's more celebrated compositions, a missing intermediary stage between the pencil drawing and the finished oil composition. In a quiet way, as befits her nature, Debo was elated: her intuition had been vindicated.

Her client was also pleased. He now not only had an important new Constable which had formerly been hidden in a cupboard; he had a saleable work of art which to an art dealer's reckoning could be worth well over £100,000.

* * *

Just as a sketch can be finished off by an artist or dealer who decides it needs 'completing', so paintings can be added to by those who think they can make them more interesting. With a picture bought in April 1985 at Sotheby's Amsterdam, Johnny Van Haeften, a Duke Street art dealer in the forefront of the international Dutch old-master market, set his colleagues reeling. He secured a major still life which most other dealers at the time had deemed too odd to consider. Sotheby's had also appeared somewhat perplexed. They had catalogued the large canvas (size 84 × 98 cm) as a work by a leading exponent of 17th-century still-life painting, Willem Claesz Heda (1594–c. 1680) but had suggested a paltry estimate of 20–25,000 guilders (£6,000–£8,000). In today's market major works by the artist have been sold for £300,000–£400,000.

The reason for the low estimate became apparent when the picture was viewed (*Fig. 11*). As it had not been illustrated in the catalogue, Johnny first saw the lot when he entered the saleroom. A connoisseur of Dutch still lives, he instantly under-stood why the price was so low. In the foreground were all the elements that he would expect from this genre of painting, and indeed from Heda in particular. It had the typical arrangement of meticulously painted food, plate and vessels, casually arranged as if left after a sumptuous banquet. It also had the stylistic features that help identify the work of Heda – a pewter jug lying as if knocked over, and a lemon with a long rind of peel hanging over the side of the table. But it was what was behind the still life that was so utterly extraordinary: a romantic landscape in lurid blues and greens. For a still life of this type, date and nationality it was the equivalent of seeing painted fairies in a Constable landscape – it was one of those things that was simply never done. Furthermore, this was the style of landscape you might find in other parts of Europe, but certainly not in 17th-century Holland. The Protestant buyers of this type of art were mostly Dutch merchants and businessmen, men of a parsimonious nature not unlike the Puritans in England, who distrusted the grand romantic statements of the Italian and French landscapists. To them, the style of this type of landscape from a Catholic climate would have been cultural anathema, and furthermore, to put it as a background to one of their meticulous still-life compositions would have been seen as at best a joke, and at worst an ill-judged affront to their sensibilities.

Johnny was bemused. He had never come across anything like this before and took out his magnifying glass to look more closely at the landscape. He was able to observe cracks running through the paint, indicating that it was certainly old. But it can't, he thought, be the same date as Heda's still life. Turning his attention to the objects on the table, he then tried to assess the painting without its backdrop. This was Heda at his best, he reflected, not only a typical composition by him but one of the first order, and in apparently excellent condition.

For the first time on one of these buying trips, Johnny's wife Sarah had come with him. Johnny now discussed the painting with her. She was also intrigued and impressed by the picture, and he put it to her that they should consider buying it for themselves: not for the gallery, for it appeared too uncertain a prospect, but as a painting to live with, however it turned out. If the background could be removed, and underneath there was the plain grey ground that he would have expected from Heda, it would represent a fabulous find. If not, then at least they would be left with an amusing, and highly decorative picture for his dining room by (at least in part) a major artist at (with luck) a relatively low cost. 'Another reason,' he added, 'was that we had recently moved to Ham near London and, well, there was a ham in it.'

Johnny and Sarah sat together during the sale. They had not actually resolved to buy the picture for certain, but when its lot number was called Johnny put up his hand at the lower estimate. As it happened, someone else had come to an optimistic view of the picture's potential as well, and the bidding soon climbed rather higher than he had expected. At 110,000 guilders (approximately £28,000) the under-bidder left off, leaving Johnny with the picture. 'We've bought it,' he said, and looked over anxiously to his wife.

The painting was shipped back to London and sent straight to the restoration studio of Patrick Corbett in Chelsea. Patrick is a specialist in 16th- and 17th-century Dutch and Flemish pictures, and he and his team of assistants are used to the exacting nature of still life — an area of old-master painting famed for its attention to magnified detail and naturalistic effects. Even he, however, had not encountered one like this before.

Carefully examining the background, he concurred with Johnny that it had to be by a different hand than the still life itself, but thought it definitely early, and possibly even 17th-century. Before Patrick started work, Johnny decided to do some further research himself. He soon came up with a fascinating but alarming point of comparison in a museum in Ghent: a 17th-century copy of the picture – which included the landscape! Whenever the landscape had been added, it therefore had to be before this copy had been executed, and because it was a 17th-century copy, that pushed the dating of the added background to close to within the artist's lifetime (he died in or around 1680). It would therefore mean removing three-hundred-year-old paint from a background close to the same period.

Patrick performed a test. With over-paint as early as this,

there is an enormous danger that it will have become fused to the original layer and therefore impossible to remove without severe damage. As he feared, the test proved negative: the paint in the background did not react to normal solvents, as is often the case with very old paint. Reluctantly, and after much deliberation, he was therefore obliged to resort to a fierce and dangerous chemical he used only rarely: dimethylformamide. Although highly effective for dissolving paint not normally removable by more orthodox means, its toxic and perilous properties are tantamount to chemical warfare and used only in extreme circumstances. Placing a protective mask around his face, Patrick poured the noxious substance from its glass bottle on to an absorbent screen of felt, which he then cantilevered an inch from the painting's surface in the area of the landscape. In this way, the solvent could only make contact with the paint surface with its fumes, and was therefore less radical and more controllable than an applied swab for the initial removal. After three days of this process the layer of landscape softened sufficiently to allow him to use the solvent neat. 'It was a terrifying job,' he recalls. 'It is a horrible chemical to use, and is a genuine danger to the restorer. For a week after I had blisters on my legs caused by an allergic reaction to the fumes.'

Patrick's health apart, they were in tremendous luck. The paint consistency of the applied landscape was slightly softer than the genuine background beneath. Working at a measured pace, Patrick was able to remove the entire added layer to reveal a near pristine grey background – and thereby return the picture to its former glory as a monochromatic masterpiece by the artist (*Fig. 12*). In the process of cleaning the lower area, they found Heda's signature on the tablecloth, together with a date of 1655 – when the artist was at the height of his powers.

Why the landscape was added, Johnny does not know – possibly it was on the eccentric whim of a 17th-century Catholic French or Italian collector, of less constrained taste, who wanted to liven up a comparatively austere Protestant work of art. As a result, however, the Van Haeftens were able to buy a masterpiece by Heda, including a ham, for their dining room at home.

'Refurbishing' does not always stop at finishing off, adding to or beautifying: it can sometimes lead to mutilation as well. Over ten years ago, David Dallas, a young art dealer working from the same premises as Richard Knight before he joined Colnaghi's, was going through a particularly frustrating period in his art-dealing career. Dave is a generalist with an innate good eye, and is equally at home with an obscure early-19th-century Welsh landscape as he is with a Renaissance nativity scene. His restless gaze will assess anything of interest and quality in a mixed sale, and over the previous year he had found at least three sleepers of consequence. All three had had depressing outcomes. Expectantly, he had shown each of them to the appropriate art historian. He had then been told, with authoritative certainty, that his paintings weren't by the artist in question. A short time after each exchange, when he had sold the pictures on for a meagre price, something had happened to change the doubting art historians' minds and they became fully accepted. He now felt he needed better luck.

Hanging high up in a routine old-master sale at Sotheby's, London in the late 1970s, Dave noticed a five-foot-high, upright painting of flowers in a vase. Around its base was a dense arrangement of seafood and vegetables (*Fig. 13*). The canvas was extremely dirty, and inaccessibly placed, but from where he stood beneath it he was impressed by its impact, in particular its 'rugged paint quality' – the confident, thick strokes which described the forms. Checking the catalogue, he saw that the picture had not been particularly rated, being described non-committally as '18th-century French school'. The estimate was £1,000–£1,500.

Without much resistance he bought it the following week for £1,700, and carried the unwieldy canvas down Bond Street to his gallery. There, Richard and Dave's assistant Melissa (Melly) Coleston examined the latest purchase with intense interest. Its extremely discoloured, yellow surface and the evident layers of paint added to the background offered a tempting prospect. Not only, they felt, might the flowers and vegetables transform in appearance when the varnish was removed, but the background looked dead in its present state. If the over-paint lifted, it could radically improve the painting's character also. They knew Dave had a talent for the recherché, and looked at it with optimism, attempting, as all dealers do in this situation, to imagine what it would be like with its outer garments of grime and paint removed.

'Let's try a test,' said Dave, as Richard, the dealer-restorer, eagerly got down his bottles of acetone and white spirit from the shelf. They placed the picture flat on the floor, its large dimensions covering the ground like a picnic rug, and Richard knelt down next to the top and applied a swab to a minute area of the background. The dirty varnish came away easily, revealing a layer of permeable-looking over-paint which also showed signs of giving way to the solvent. The chemical mixture seemed correctly balanced, there appeared to be little risk of damaging the original paint beneath, and Dave, although aware of the extreme dangers of allowing inexperienced people to use solvents, felt sufficiently confident in this case to suggest they all had a go. And so it was that, under Richard's supervision, the three of them crouched on the floor, swabs in hand, tackling different sides of the painting.

'I had a go at the cauliflower,' Dave recalls. 'Melly took on the right-hand background, and Richard took the flowers.' In no time at all the floor became covered with soiled, discarded swabs, soaked in the thick layer of varnish and added paint that continued to come away freely from the surface of the canvas. The task was enrapturing: the process of taking off dirt and over-paint to reveal a genuine old work beneath ranks amongst the most therapeutic actions known to man, and they would happily have continued had not Melly brought the proceedings to an abrupt halt with a small shriek: 'My God, there's a face here!' Both men stopped what they were doing and crawled hurriedly to her side of the picture. Sure enough, protruding in from the right, next to the vase of flowers, was a life-sized human head half showing through the semi-removed over-paint.

They looked at each other in disbelief and then back at the head. 'I remember thinking it could only be one thing,' Dave recalled. 'Looking at where the face came in, it appeared to terminate abruptly through the cheek where the canvas ended – indicating that we were dealing with a cut-down from a larger canvas.' 'Cut-downs' are a not uncommon occurrence in the commercial art world. Either to fit a picture into a particular space, a smaller room or simply to salvage a more attractive passage from an otherwise undesirable picture, in the last few hundred years countless works have been butchered to satisfy the whims and requirements of their owners.

For Dave it was a sad outcome; the picture had been cleaning so well, but with part of its composition so rudely missing, it could never now be viewed as a serious commercial prospect. Unknown to them, however, the missing part of the original picture – to which this flower piece crucially related – was closer to hand than they ever could have imagined at the time. 'We patched it up,' said Dave, 'put back the over-paint to make it look respectable, and I then tried to sell it within the trade as a merely decorative picture – explaining that it was a fragment of something larger.' With a re-varnish, they were able to return the painting to a cleaner-looking version of its former appearance, and he consigned it to another dealer, asking to be returned £3,000. But despite reducing the price more and more over the succeeding two years, Dave still found it on his hands, by which time, needing the money, he was prepared to take £1,500 – and therefore a loss. 'It passed from dealer to dealer, I heard later,' said Dave, 'but no one seemed to have any luck with this rather blighted picture.' He then re-entered it in a Christie's sale and received a pleasant surprise. The cataloguer had a high view of that painting's quality, and attributed it to a 17th-century Italian painter called Andrea Belvedere, with an estimate of £4,000–£6,000. But Dave still had serious doubts about the saleability of the picture, and when he telephoned the salerooms on the evening of the sale, shortly before he was to head off for his home in Wales, he was quite prepared to hear that it had been 'bought in' or remained unsold. He spoke to a man in the accounts department.

'Lot 23, attributed to Andrea Belvedere,' came back the voice at the end of the line, 'Yes, that made £35,000.'

'You've got that wrong,' said Dave, 'it's the painting consigned by Anthony Dallas & Son.'

'That's right,' he reaffirmed, '£35,000.'

Dave was understandably thrilled, but equally confused. How on earth could the picture have made so much, after two years of touting it throughout the trade without result, and at a fraction of that price? He rang up a friend who had been at the sale, but he was not able to add much except to say that two Italians appeared to be 'grudge bidding' against each other – a more aggressive form of 'bitch bidding' in which the adversaries are trying to settle a score – but that it was finally Jackie King, a well-known London auction agent who acts anonymously on behalf of major dealers and collectors, who secured it with a bid on top.

The buyer was in fact an international dealer called Silvano Lodi, Dave found out much later. He next saw his picture illustrated on two pages of colour in *Natura Morta Italiana*, a book on the major still-life paintings of 17th-century Italy, where it was featured as arguably the most important still-life painting by the leading late 16th- and 17th-century Genoese painter, Bernardo Strozzi (1581–1644). Not, however, that one would have instantly recognised it after the massive transformation that had taken place (*Fig. 14*).

The picture had been cleaned to reveal the figure on the right holding, it turned out, a bowl of cherries. The most astonishing thing of all was that the missing lateral part had not been discarded, but had been found, conveniently within reach. The hacked-off strip had been placed on its side and attached to the top of the canvas where it had been painted over to raise the background behind the vase – no doubt a cheap way to adapt the picture, requiring no new canvas (*Fig. 15*). Not only did this strip contain the rest of the body, it added to the still life a brace of hanging birds which can be seen to the right of the girl. Why it had been done one can only speculate: to fit a particular space? To make it look like a more conventional flower piece? To pass it off as the work of another artist? The changes must have been made at least a hundred years ago, and we are never likely to know the answer. Lodi, however, experienced in the still lives of Strozzi, presumably recognised the picture's true authorship from the picture as it was presented. All David knew was that, had he, Richard and Melly continued their cleaning that afternoon, he would have made the discovery himself and become the owner of a major Italian picture. But due to the misapprehension that he was uncovering a fragment, the painting could now be added to his list of fouled-up commercial opportunities, as another coup that at the last moment had slipped his grasp.

The painting had thus been turned from a horizontal painting of a girl with flowers into an upright flower and vegetable piece, conforming more to the conventional appearance of a still life. In the process of mutilation, its authorship had been obscured for future generations, changing it from a picture which in today's market could make £500,000 or more, into something which for a time quite literally nobody wanted.

* * *

It is not only artistry which later painters and restorers seek to change, but human appearances as well. The infamous turn-of-the-century art dealer Joseph Duveen diligently prettified faces to make them appeal to his clientele. Renaissance Madonnas would lose their rounded features in favour of more up-to-date models; Flemish visages of the late 15th century, portrayed with a look of gaunt distinction, would develop more modern sex appeal; idiosyncratic-looking men would be rendered more conventionally handsome. Interestingly, it is often only possible to detect these alterations, if cleverly executed, when you are no longer in the period in which they were adapted. When, say, a 1930s artist or faker attempted to alter or disguise a Renaissance picture, although unknown to him, he would execute the changes with a 1930s mindset and a 1930s concept of beauty. Hilariously, therefore, you can sometimes spot a face that has been enhanced or beautified during that period because it has taken on the faintly perceptible facial traits of the likes of Joan Crawford or Errol Flynn.

Four years ago, at a sale of British pictures in London, I came across a rather extraordinary-looking portrait of a lady, described as having been traditionally identified as the Countess of Carnarvon. It was catalogued as 'Circle of Sir Anthony Van Dyck (1599–1641)', and showed an elaborately dressed seated lady, wearing a mauve robe and running a garland of roses through her hands. The estimate was £4,000–£7,000 (*Fig. 16*). Although the auction house had clearly regarded it as a 17th-century work, they had not deemed it to be of sufficiently high quality to be by an artist of the stature of Van Dyck. To 20th-century eyes, the portrait was not without its selling-points: the lady's voluminous mauve costume was unusually sumptuous for a 17th-century British image; the jewellery and flowers also added charm, and its large size ($45\frac{1}{2} \times 34\frac{1}{4}$ inches) and colour gave it impact. As it was not by Van Dyck, however, these features turned it into a 'decorative' rather than serious work of art.

I went down to see the painting about two weeks before the sale, when it was propped against a bench in the basement waiting to be hung. With a bright light and an ultraviolet lamp at my disposal, I then subjected her to merciless scrutiny. The overhead lights were turned off and, running the ultraviolet beam over the portrait's surface, I soon realised that there were large swathes of over-paint, particularly in the background and beneath the figure's neck. Using the normal lamp on the same areas, I confirmed the diagnosis by noticing that cracks which ran through the woman's upper facial features and body were not present in these over-painted areas. Mentally marking these differing passages of paint, I then asked for the overhead light to be turned on again. It had been a clever job, executed with a high degree of professionalism, but looking with re-educated eyes at the picture as a whole, I could see that much of it was later, and almost certainly 20th-century. And yet despite all this later wrapping, the expression in the upper part of her face remained bright, constant and unsullied, as if the poor lady were oblivious to her predicament. Furthermore, the parts that were not over-painted had the qualities of fine observation and painterly skill – sufficiently so, in fact, to be by the master himself.

On returning to my gallery, I took out a monograph on the works of Van Dyck. Using the image in the sale catalogue, and attempting to will away what I now considered to be later editions, I then turned the pages of the book in search of the same face. It was not until I arrived at the glossary of works considered to be 'after Van Dyck', in other words copies, that I came across what had to be the same woman. Although the overall composition was a little different – her dress had altered in shape and colour and she was no longer holding a garland – the same face sat upon the shoulders of a portrait labelled as 'Countess Dysart'. Identifying the figure as the Countess of Carnarvon, it now appeared, had been a figment of someone's imagination, and to this day I have no idea why the painting had assumed that name. Compared to the picture at auction, the face was plumper around the chin, but recalling that that was one of the areas over-painted in the auction picture, I was certain it had to be the same sitter. Looking her up in our reference books, I soon discovered she was a not insignificant historical figure. She lived at Ham House in Richmond near London during the Civil War, and was famed for using her guile and courage to prevent her home being seized by Cromwell's troops while her husband, a Royalist, was in attendance to the King. Reading further, I gained the impression that she was viewed by her contemporaries as something of a heroine – at one point during the Civil War penetrating enemy lines to make contact with her husband.

The magnificent 17th-century Ham House, famed for its furnishings and near original layout, is open to the public, and I went to visit that weekend. Upstairs in a gallery filled with portraits in opulent gilded frames, hanging above a discreet lift shaft, much to my excitement I encountered her again (*Fig. 17*). Not only was it the same woman, but the very same composition, and described on a label beneath as 'after Van Dyck', in other words a copy. The two pictures were identical except for three differences: the Ham portrait had an elaborate stone shelf upon which the roses rested – the other had a simple ledge; here the Countess's left hand was draped in a white sleeve, in the other it was partially rolled back to reveal more red satin; and, most poignantly, the lady above me sported an ample double chin, giving the other, by contrast, the appearance of having had radical plastic surgery. The comparison both amazed and fazed me, and I went looking round the house for more information, at first unable to process my findings.

I managed to obtain some notes on the history of the pictures from the administrator's office downstairs and soon established that the portrait had been described as 'after Van Dyck' as early as the 17th century, unequivocally indicating that there therefore had to be a Van Dyck from which it was copied. It seems so clear now in retrospect, but it took me at least a day to piece together my various observations and come up with the obvious deduction that the painting at auction, beneath its cloak of later paint, showed sufficient qualities in the areas that were exposed to be a contender for that as yet unlocated original. But it had been so heavily adapted by a later hand as to be now virtually unrecognisable.

I went to the auction the following week, giving myself a limit of £20,000, which although perhaps a fifth of the value of an original work of this type, reflected a lingering degree of doubt. My sincere hope was that beneath all the over-painting I would not only find a genuine picture, but one in salvageable condition. But I could not count on either with certainty. I knew it was a gamble, and although the risks had been lessened by research, I had to remain sensible to the fact that the chance of restoration revealing a picture in fine condition was far from sure.

It was a well-attended sale and, although prices were high for all the more decorative and important pictures, there seemed little interest in the strange-looking lady. Much to my delight, there was only one other bidder, on the telephone, who lost interest at £8,500. Lady Dysart thus became my property for a price which, quite frankly, reflected her ungainly appearance.

I took the picture that night to the restoration studio of Patrick Corbett, who has worked on many Van Dycks in private English collections over the last twenty years, and relishes a restoration challenge. He greeted it with curiosity, placed it on the easel, and directed his searingly bright studio lights on to the canvas. He then reached for his magnifying lenses and, strapping them to his head, focused first on Lady Dysart's left shoulder, in the area which differed from the Ham picture with its turned-up satin sleeve. 'This paint seems different from the rest of the dress,' he announced. Although this area had not shown up under the ultraviolet rays, very early over-paint does not, owing to fluorescence fading over a long period, and I had been unable to make up my mind whether or not this was a later addition or a variant on the original design. Looking closely now at the brushstrokes, I realised that the technique was slicker here than in the rest of her gown and therefore by a different hand – although it still had *craquelure* running through it, testifying to its great age. I then handed Patrick a photograph of the Ham picture. 'Interesting,' he said. 'If this picture has been altered, and I think it has, then the shoulder area was done by a different artist only a few years later – it's 17th-century paint.' Gulping somewhat at the prospect of having to remove paint that was added only a few years after the painting's completion, I asked him to move to a safer area – that of the Countess's nipped and tucked chin, which looked even more ludicrously cosmetic under the fierce light. Focusing hard on her throat, Patrick then took a small swab of cotton wool, wound it on to a stick, and dipped it into a ready mixed solvent. 'We'll go very slowly to begin with,' he said, and leaned forward to apply the solvent.

Nothing happened on his first attempts, so he increased the concentration and reapplied it, leaving it no more than a few seconds to act. The white swab then picked up a trace of pink: the paint was lifting. 'There she goes,' he murmured as the solvent bit deeper, and a new surface began to appear. At first it was difficult to see what was going on, because the tonality of the revealed paint beneath was not very different to the layer above. He started with a single square centimetre, but slowly, over the next three-quarters of an hour, an extra fold of flesh took shape, gaining the coherence of a chin. From beneath the dissolving, tacky surface fell a voluptuous roll of soft, white skin, gently modulated with light shadow. With it, the whole effect of the face changed. The Countess's pinched, neurotic demeanour gave way to one of well-fed composure. The shrill, implausible features which were attempting to evoke a 20th-century pin-up were now replaced by those of a full-faced, determined 17th-century Royalist who could face a Roundhead without a tremble. The head of the formidable chatelaine of Ham had resurfaced.

Her dress was a very different prospect. Recovering hardened 17th-century paint from beneath another 17th-century layer, as has been shown, can present an extraordinarily difficult task for a restorer. The restoration of Van Haeften's Heda was possible because the differing properties of the paint used allowed one to be dissolved from the other. These layers, however, were virtually the same. Patrick began by taking an x-ray to confirm our hypothesis, and, as we suspected, beneath the crimson additions were flowing white robes that conformed precisely to the image at Ham House. It was now just a question of getting to them without damaging this original paint. A test showed that solvents were out. Anything strong enough to dissolve the top layer would do the same to the one beneath. The only alternative was a scalpel. Fortunately, there was a level of discoloured varnish between the crimson and the white paint, indicating that who-ever had painted the changes on to the dress had not cleaned off the picture's varnish before doing so. This had an unforeseen benefit for the 20th-century restorer, for Patrick was able to use this discoloured layer as a 'buffer zone' – chipping away with a scalpel but stopping whenever he encountered this dividing layer of yellow varnish.

Working over two months, with menacingly sharp blades, members of Patrick's team gradually divested the Countess of her later garment. It required such intense concentration that an hour was the most that each could do at one sitting. In order to cope, the added area of fabric was squared up with chalk, and his team worked in shifts, each person doing one square inch at a time. The shelf beneath proved to be a 19th-century addition, not as recent as the re-painting of the face, but easily removable with solvents to reveal the simpler ledge beneath.

Two months later work on the picture was completed. From beneath all the many additions a fully authentic Van Dyck then reappeared (*Fig. 18*). Taking into account all the circumstances, it had to be the same picture which had been copied in the 17th century, the copy now hanging at Ham. Whether it was there originally, no one can say with certainty, for much of the picture's early history is unknown.

And why the changes to conceal the Countess's original identity and appearance? Her dress was updated in the late 17th century, probably to conform to then more fashionable baroque styles in contemporary costume. The changes had the effect of breaking up the classical line and sweep seen in dresses of the previous epoch, to be replaced by the fuller look favoured in the later Stuart period. The shelf was painted to give more decorative appeal — an incongruous *trompe l'oeil* effect probably added in the late Victorian period out of ignorance or dislike of Van Dyck's more straightforward solution. The changes to her face were a simple cosmetic 'improvement', datable to the first thirty years of this century and created by an individual and a time which rated the sharper looks of Vivien Leigh and her contemporaries above those of a stalwart mid-17th-century aristocrat. Thus encumbered by the improvements of fashion, the Countess struggled, unrecognised, to auction.

I subsequently sold her to a collector of 17th-century painting who was delighted to acquire an original Van Dyck, although one perhaps not quite so languid and elegant as many of his other portraits. As with the Lawrence portrait of Angerstein in the previous chapter, confidentiality unfortunately prevents me from revealing for how much — but the sale of both paintings did go some way towards covering other purchases made in those years that did not end so happily.

CHAPTER THREE

All Places At All Times

THERE EXISTS IN the art world a certain type of dealer who does not work from a gallery but prefers instead to travel incessantly, covering the auction houses of the country, and acting as a link between London and the far reaches of the trade. Often described rather crudely as 'runners', these are the middle-men, dealers who will also act as agents, bringing to the capital paintings that are more keenly sought-after, and therefore more highly valued there than they are in the country.

Within this fascinating stratum of the art world one of these roving dealers reigns supreme. He is Philip Archibald Reginald Parker, but owing to an obscure epithet bestowed on him by his sister when a three-year-old, he is known to his wife, friends and fellow dealers as 'Buffy'. It is a name well known in the art world, not only because of Buffy's indefatigable energy which carries him to auction houses across Britain every week, but through a number of art finds, and one in particular that has gone down in the annals of the commercial art world as perhaps the most spectacular in living memory. It was a rightful reward, and an example of how opportunity can be created by taking

infinite pains to be at all places at all times or, to use an appropriate metaphor from fishing – Buffy is a keen angler himself – the
longer you keep your fly in the water, the greater the chance of
catching fish.

Buffy lives with his wife and four children in an expansive,
Jacobean-style country house in Hampshire a short distance from
the river Test. In the cellar beneath, adapted from extensive
Victorian slate wine bins, is a superbly organised storage system
reaching far into the darkness, with innumerable paintings, traversing every subject in art from Manchester street scenes to
Venetian canal views, from landscapes with sheep to German
hunting dogs at the kill. By his own admission, most of them
are 'decorative' works – an art-dealing term implying that their
merits are to please, rather than particularly to impress by their
quality or authorship. But then that is the nature of much of his
business. For Buffy is by temperament irrepressibly acquisitive,
and he has turned this tendency, aided by his astutely commercial
eye, into a highly successful business which feeds a large section
of the art world with an unabating supply of pictures from his
clearing house in Hampshire.

A rival art dealer once caught sight of Buffy's work diary, and
was awestruck. For Buffy's home is the centre of operations for
a business that, once understood and observed, leaves most other
art dealers feeling physically inadequate. It starts on Sunday
night when he sits down and goes through the coming week's
country-sale catalogues, which he receives at the rate of about
twenty a day, and attempts to make sense of descriptions that
usually consist of no more than a few words and are rarely illustrated. He is therefore obliged to make instinctual judgements,
combining his knowledge of the auction and the area together
with clues drawn from other objects in the sale. The real slog
starts on Monday when he will try and fit in up to eight viewings
of the more interesting sales; by the end of the week he will have
travelled perhaps a further thousand miles, viewed about five

Fig. 1. A cross-section of paint from an 18th-century English picture. Beneath the top layer of dirty varnish are different layers of paint, denoting changes of the artist's mind and build-up of primer on the canvas.

Fig. 2. The eyes of the Lady in the 'Detroit Van Dyck' at auction, showing build-up of discoloured varnish.

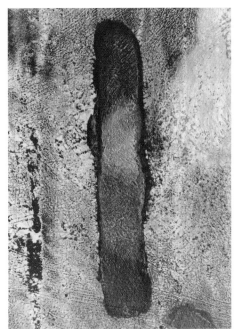

Fig. 4. (*above, left*) Portrait of *John Julius Angerstein* at auction when catalogued as 'Circle of Sir Thomas Lawrence'.

Fig. 5. (*above, right*) A test showing a curl from Angerstein's hair, formerly painted out.

Fig. 6. (*right*) *John Julius Angerstein* by Sir Thomas Lawrence, by kind permission of Lloyd's of London.

Fig. 3. (*previous page*) The 'Detroit' Van Dyck fully cleaned, restored and authenticated.

Fig. 7. The Angerstein head sketch by Lawrence, now fully cleaned.

Fig. 8. (*left*) An example of over-paint on a restored 17th-century Dutch portrait, fluorescing under an ultraviolet beam.

Fig 9. (*below, right*) A close-up of the over-painted sky in the Constable sketch, showing a cleaning test.

Fig. 10. (*bottom*) The cleaned sketch: A study for *Valley Farm* by John Constable.

Fig. 11. The Willem Claesz Heda when at auction.

Fig. 12. The Heda returned to its original appearance.

Fig. 13. (*above, left*) The Bernardo Strozzi before cleaning and restoration.
Fig. 14. (*above, right*) The Strozzi stripped of its later paint to reveal the 'missing' fragment.
Fig. 15. (*below*) The Strozzi revived (private collection).

Fig. 16. (*above, left*) The 'Circle of Van Dyck' at auction with a tentative identification of Countess of Carnarvon.

Fig. 17. (*above, right*) *Countess of Dysart*: a copy after Van Dyck at Ham House (detail).

Fig. 18. *Countess of Dysart* by Sir Anthony Van Dyck.

thousand pictures, covered about twenty more auction rooms, and will have acquired anything up to forty more canvases.

Particularly in the South of England, Buffy is therefore probably the best known man in the auction world. But this is not without hazards. He now has to employ porters or friends to execute bids on his behalf because local dealers have been known to 'run him up' – either following his proven commercial instincts or, more sinisterly, deliberately bidding against him out of spite. 'Bitch bidding', as it is known, is when disgruntled rivals – who in country sales are usually the local trade – use gratuitous bids deliberately to push up the victim, making him pay more than he need. And the minefield does not end there either. There is the auctioneer himself who will almost certainly 'run' a bidder up to the reserve in a practice known as 'taking bids off the wall' both in an attempt to ensure the lot is sold and also to create the impression of furious bidding which will hopefully encourage others into thinking they might be missing a bargain. An almost failsafe method for bypassing this commercial battlefield altogether is to consign confidential bids to a saleroom porter, or a friend who can act as a decoy. Using this technique, and apparently limitless stamina, Buffy has been known to return home with up to two thousand pictures a year.

Regularly, from all parts of the art world, including Japan, dealers visit Buffy's country house to inspect his ever-changing stock. Most of it he will sell immediately, usually to London dealers; some he will consign to other traders on a sale-or-return basis, but about a quarter he will take up to the auction rooms, particularly Christie's and Bonhams, where his visits are something of an event – the appropriate expert in charge being drawn from his office into the street to survey Buffy's wares from the back of his car. Since 1988, when the name Buffy Parker became synonymous with one of the most glamorous discoveries in the modern art world, the telephone call from reception to announce the arrival of Mr Parker has had a Pavlovian effect on some specialists, hungry to view the next consignment from the country. For this celebrated discovery elevated Parker from the level of hard-working runner to the status of art-dealing celebrity overnight and, in commercial terms, made him one of the stars of his profession. It wasn't always so.

Although from a hallowed dynasty himself – Buffy is closely related to the Earl of Macclesfield – it became quite clear from an early age that he was to eschew the safe route. His father a Royal photographer, his mother Una-Mary Parker, a journalist and now successful author, the family blood already coursed away from convention, and Buffy continued in the flow. At the age of sixteen he went to acting school in Chiswick, taking advantage of the gift he has for looking youthful – at eighteen he appeared to be fourteen – and even now at forty appears five years younger, with albeit thinning blond hair and crisply carved English features. But needing a second living up his sleeve, at eighteen he took a job as a porter at Bonhams and, taking well to the milieu, after a few years was promoted to Gallery Manager of Paintings. Four years later he felt his indentures were done, left his acting aspirations behind him, his auction career also, and embarked on a then uncertain future, in which he now excels.

It was in early summer of 1987 and Buffy, at the time based in London, was going through his now established routine of sifting through auction catalogues. He picked up one from Sotheby's, who in those days had a Chester auction house – a grand provincial outpost, mimicking in many ways the activities of its Bond Street headquarters, but dealing in lower-quality lots, particularly from the north-west of England. One item abruptly caught his attention. It was Lot No. 4182 on the third day of a series of sales selling everything from jukeboxes to old masters, and it was buried anonymously in the picture section. Described as '19th-century Italian school, a portrait of Pope Clement VII', with dimensions of 40 × 36 inches, what especially alerted him were the words that followed it: 'on slate'. Another attractive aspect was its estimate – a paltry £200–£300. Buffy could only remember seeing a very few pictures painted on slate. He might have sold one, he couldn't really remember, but certainly not of this size. Trying to visualise a piece of stone 3½ feet by 3 feet, it struck him that a painting of this weight and substance was highly unusual for what he inferred to be a 19th-century copy – for he recalled that Pope Clement VII was a 16th-century figure. He ringed the lot, and inked a Chester trip into his diary for the end of the week.

Chester from London was a morning's run, so he left early to beat the local traffic, allowing time to view the sale before the lots came up in the afternoon. He arrived in good time and made his way to the auction rooms in Watergate Street, the picturesque medieval centre of Chester, where Sotheby's had chosen to locate their north-west frontier. The trade, Buffy recalls, was out in force – the art world was booming, and in those days interesting sales had about them the atmosphere of battle. Art prices were rising steadily, new records were being created each week, and for an astute dealer there were always opportunities to profit from the market's giddy progress. The auction room was congested.

Buffy had a cursory look around the walls, and although his eye was delayed by the odd interesting lot, he was more concerned to locate the picture that had earlier that week captured his imagination in the catalogue. He moved around the crowded room, taking notes on other pictures that appealed to his commercial eye – 19th-century landscapes, portraits and old-master copies – and just as he began to think that his Pope on slate had been withdrawn, he noticed the back of a shallow wooden crate, leaning against a table, about fifteen feet from the auctioneer's rostrum. He walked round to the front and looked inside.

Framed by the pine borders of the crate, and heavily glazed

by a thick layer of grime which half-filtered the image beneath, he was confronted by the readable form of a seated figure in a scarlet hat and robe, edged with thin strips of yellowed white fur (*Fig. 19*). Although darkened by the accumulated dirt of time, Buffy was able clearly to make out the firm, olive-brown, three-quarter profile of the Pope, with a long beard melting into shadowy obscurity beneath his chin. His eye was instantly drawn by the exquisitely depicted gold and encrusted rings on his fingers, and then by the naturally slumped and relaxed pose, which despite its bulk had a look of grace and authority. Behind the Pope's chair he could just make out the gloomy shape of drapery and a column, barely discernible through the grime. Hands, which often present a complex anatomical challenge to an artist, are usually an indication of quality in a picture of this type, and here they were exquisitely described and drawn, adding an extra dimension of character to the portrayal.

Not a man who wastes his words on hyperbole, Buffy today recalls that the impact of the picture was physical: 'It hit me around the back of the head. To me, this had no chance of being 19th-century. I decided resolutely there and then that I was going to go home with it.'

So powerful was the presence before him, Buffy was then consumed by a fit of nerves. He looked tentatively around the room and noticed amongst the assembly of traders two West End old-master dealers, but neither of them, as far as he could detect, seemed particularly aware of the picture, nor of Buffy himself surveying it. He then tried to clear his head and assess the work objectively. Could this be a lost work by a Renaissance master like Raphael? Surely, he reflected, someone must have checked it out. He looked again at the image, this time more analytically. Oddly, he thought, it seemed to have been painted straight on to the slate – there did not appear to have been any primer used to cover the stone, thereby giving the artist a smoother surface on to which to apply the later paint strokes.

This is normal with works on canvas or panel, and its absence aroused slight suspicion. Could he be looking at a very clever 19th-century or later copy, produced by a faker well versed in the techniques of Renaissance painting, but who had forgotten to include this basic trait? Often, however, it is common sense that provides the supportive or dissuasive argument in the assessment of such things, and Buffy asked himself why a faker would go to the highly unorthodox lengths of painting on slate? Canvas or panel perhaps, but not this most unlikely of all supports. The slate was around half an inch thick and the painting, he realised as he levered it half out of the crate, was almost too heavy for a man to lift on his own. Peering down the back, he saw no labels or marks to give him further clues. Although a prodigious generalist, Buffy did not sell early Italian paintings on slate every day. He therefore had to rely on instinct, and it told him, loud and clear, that this picture had to be bought.

The picture was due to come up later that day and Buffy spent his time perusing the other lots, doing his best to forget the Pope until its moment came. Whatever the outcome of his bid for the Pope, he would go home that day with six pictures of the type that formed the staple diet of his business – copies and commercial images for the decorative side of the West End trade. The Pope came up mid-afternoon, and as the auctioneer progressed towards it, dispatching the previous lots with great speed, Buffy's mouth began to go dry. Pictures are often withdrawn at the last moment when, for varying reasons, the department or vendor decides against selling. One of the main causes, in this sort of sale, is if the experts in charge suddenly feel that a lot has been under-catalogued, to which they are sometimes alerted if cognizant buyers show exclusive interest. Buffy had half expected that this might have happened here, and was therefore immensely relieved to hear the Pope's lot number, 4182, announced to the room. His heart pounding, adrenalin flowing, he then braced himself for action.

At this stage he had no idea what he was prepared to go to. He just knew he wanted the picture. The bidding opened at £150. No hands were raised, so Buffy lifted his and took it to £160. The auctioneer looked down at his notes and came back with £170. Buffy now knew he was either bidding against a deposited bid or, more likely, against the reserve price set by the auctioneer before the auction – normally about ten per cent below the lower of the two estimates – and decided to raise it to £180. As he suspected, lacking any more reserve, the auction-eer's eyes left the rostrum and panned the room for more buyers. None seemed forthcoming. Seconds of intense pain went by as he continued to fish for bids. Buffy pleaded for the gavel to go down, risking a glance at the two West End old-master dealers, but they appeared distracted in conversation. Mercy was then granted. Wood struck wood. Buffy's name was logged by the clerk. The Pope was his.

Buffy's first reaction was to think he had bought the wrong lot. He quite simply could not believe it. What particularly amazed him was the price – the lowest possible given his assump-tion that he was bidding against reserve: not one person in the room, West End dealer or casual punter, had lifted their finger in competition. He looked at the label on the crate to reassure himself that it was the right lot number. It was. The sale was now rattling along, and with the solid realisation that he really had bought the picture, a feeling of intense relief and security settled upon him. But Buffy's sense of disbelief was soon replaced by more practical considerations. No one else had recognised the Pope as an important painting, so it was now up to him to prove his hunch, to disprove the prevailing disregard from auction house and fellow dealers, and convince the art world, with all its lucrative consequences, that he had found a Renaissance masterpiece.

Late that night in his drawing room in London, Buffy wetted

a swab of cotton wool with white spirit, and touched the top left corner of the slate. Applying white spirit to the surface of a matt and dirty picture like this can have the same impact as running your finger along a misted window. For as long as the area you've wiped remains clear, you can see through to the forms and colours beneath. Temporarily rejuvenating that area of the painting's varnish in this way, he was able to create a small window in the grime, and through it showed a vibrant green, as startling as a pane of lit stained glass, indicating the colour that would emerge with cleaning. It was rarely Buffy's policy to clean pictures, for he knew full well that dealers and auctioneers generally prefer the untouched artefact, but he had thereby gained a further assurance of its quality. The white spirit began to evaporate, returning the area to obscurity, and Buffy now felt that he had procured enough initial information to start his researches. Tomorrow, he resolved, would not be a day spent on the road, but in the Witt Art Library, where somewhere, amongst the innumerable photographs of paintings across the world, he might find a further piece of evidence to affirm his hunches.

Before he set off for Portman Square the next morning he decided to ring the auction house in Chester and speak to the department who had catalogued it. There had been no provenance published in the catalogue, and as there were no labels or inscriptions on the reverse, however fragmentary, he hoped he might gain some information from the cataloguer. He thought it very unlikely that Sotheby's would reveal the name of the vendor, but there might be something that would give him a lead in establishing its history. Often a touch circumspect when telephoned by a dealer the day after a sale and questioned about a work that has sold for very little, a member of the department answered who was nevertheless helpful. Unable to say who had consigned the Pope, the cataloguer did mention that there had been a label on the reverse which might prove useful. 'A label?'

Buffy asked, amazed. Had there been a label of any description, he would have surely seen it. The label, he was then told, described the painting as an important work from the collection of the Earls of Pembroke, and had since become detached from the picture. It had also, presumably, identified the Pope as Clement VII. Had they rated the picture seriously, Buffy surmised, more effort would have been made to find or preserve this document — as it was, for a low-value old master such as this, the department was not losing too much sleep. Armed with a Polaroid snap of the picture and the new information about its provenance, Buffy set off for the Witt.

Every Western picture of any consequence that has been photographed in the last fifty years has a good chance of ending up in this voluminous photographic library attached to the Courtauld Institute. In many ways it is the heart and lungs of the art business, and every week day is attended by art students, dealers and auctioneers in search of evidence, comparison and information. Green and red boxes line an acreage of wall space, each filled with mounted photographs from museums, libraries, private collections, auction catalogues and publications. Initially daunting, the reading tables of the library have nevertheless marked the scenes of some of the greatest revelations in the business, as those who know how to work the system manage to locate the lost image or necessary comparison to clinch an attribution.

Buffy sat down and, choosing to approach the task by a process of elimination, made a list of the five greatest artists who could have painted this portrait, starting with Raphael. Struck by his memory of the iridescent background colour glimpsed during the white-spirit test the night before, he included a number of leading Venetian painters renowned for their rich pigments, and listed Titian, Veronese, Giorgione and del Piombo. In the Witt the boxes for each artist are divided into categories relating to subject, so he narrowed down his search by looking for portraits of Pope Clement and, more broadly, seated single figures with hands. By commencing the search in this way, he would be able to discount each possible artist within twenty minutes, and if necessary cover a score of them by lunchtime. He took down the boxes, two at a time, and got to work.

He quickly discounted Raphael. Although there were stylistic similarities he could not find anything of comparable severity or classicism. There was one portrait of Pope Julius II with which there was close comparison but not enough to permit him to attribute his Pope to the same master. Making his way through the other boxes, it wasn't until he reached the final artist in his first hitlist of five, Sebastiano del Piombo, that he scented his quarry. In the box was a file specifically devoted to portraits by del Piombo of Clement VII. He turned back the cardboard cover and was met by Clement's now familiar face, but without a beard, painted by the artist when the Pope was manifestly younger. It hung in the Museo Nazionale di Capodimonte in Naples. Beneath this was another image of a del Piombo portrait from the Kunsthistorisches Museum in Vienna. This time the similarities to his Chester find were remarkable. Painted with a beard, from the same angle, there seemed to be unmistakable links, not only facially, but also in the handling of the drapery. Buffy flipped rapidly through the remaining images, some of which he noticed were on slate, and amongst duplicate photographs of the first two found a further work, a double portrait of the Pope with Charles V, which resided in the Galleria Nazionale in Parma. Del Piombo and Clement were clearly artist and patron – del Piombo probably being the Pope's official portrait painter – and taking into account the stylistic similarities, Buffy's portrait seemed to fit convincingly into the artist's oeuvre. But there were no references to a picture of the Pope in a past collection of the Earls of Pembroke; his picture, it appeared, was an unknown variant, and to be fully accepted would have to pass academic scrutiny and adjudication. Aware of the task ahead, but elated

by the magnificence of his mounting evidence, Buffy set about
the next stage in the process of discovery. He now knew that he
did not have a work by the greatest of them all, Raphael, but
there was a high chance that he could prove it was by one of the
rarest and most acclaimed artists of the following generation: the
friend and contemporary of Michelangelo, Sebastiano Luciani,
called del Piombo because of an illustrious office conferred on
him by Pope Clement. Furthermore, Clement himself was arguably the most significant Pope in British history, the Pontiff who
forbade Henry VIII's divorce from Catherine of Aragon – an
action which ultimately led to England's break from Rome.
Artist and sitter combined had enormous commercial and art-
historical significance.

As he had bought the painting at Sotheby's, out of tact and
good sense Buffy decided to employ the services of Christie's in
the next stage of its authentication and ultimate sale. Later that
week he made an appointment with Gregory Martin, one of their
chief old-master directors, and drove the picture round to their
auction house in King Street, London. For the last few years
both major auction houses have had small, discreet booths close
to the front counter where specialists and their clients, after the
initial encounter, can disappear off to be alone with a work of
art. A light goes on above the door, indicating that they are not
to be disturbed, and the work is then confidentially discussed
and assessed. And so it was in the summer of 1987 that Buffy
found himself with Martin and the Pope, discussing a picture
which could change his life.

Martin wiped the picture over with white spirit, more exten-
sively than Buffy had done earlier that week, and was instantly
seduced by the picture's outstanding colouring and quality. He
recalls asking Buffy whether it had any provenance or history.
Great works of art rarely, if ever, escape history's regard and a
picture such as this, if it were in an 18th-century or earlier
British collection, would at least have been referred to in print

by some connoisseur or historian. Even a mention in an inventory helps establish that a picture has been around since that time, a vital aid for authentication, and can even lead to conclusive evidence of authorship. It has even happened that receipts, from the very artist who painted a particular picture, have been found languishing in family archives.

Buffy related to Martin how he had been reliably informed that a label had once been attached to the back of the slate which had linked it to the family of the Earls of Pembroke. Martin then left the booth, and returned ten minutes later with an early Christie's catalogue, dated 6th May 1851. It was for the sale of the collection of the Earl of Pembroke at Carlton House Terrace in London. On the second day of the dispersal of the Earl's extensive and celebrated collection was Lot No. 181, a picture of the following description: 'S. del Piombo: Portrait of Leo X, seated in his robe'. The picture was unsold at 180 guineas, but ten years later came back to another sale at Christie's, when it was described again as Pope Leo, but now as a work on slate. This time it made 295 guineas. Although identified as Pope Leo, the fact that it was described as being on slate, and bearing in mind that with the passage of time the identities of portraits are often confused, Martin felt sure that it had to be the same painting. The attribution to del Piombo, not the most obvious attribution for an old master in the 19th century, was a further indicator. Buffy was now also convinced. Both had been struck firstly and most significantly by the portrait's quality. Next it had worked academically, fitting perfectly into the context of the other known portraits of the Pope and, if anything, was more monumental than the rest, suggesting a work of prime quality. (But this would not be fully determined until cleaning.) Finally, the fact that it came from the Earl's collection not only gave it crucial provenance but a certain historical stature as well.

It was now left to Gregory Martin to take the painting to the next and final stage of authentication, to be scrutinised by the man who had made del Piombo his chosen subject, and whose pronouncements on authenticity were of critical importance. Every great artist has at least one representative on earth, whose job it is to sort the wheat from the chaff – the work of copyists, pastiche artists and emulators from that of the original artist. In the case of del Piombo, it was an Englishman, at the time sojourning in Italy for six weeks, who would be able to provide the final pronouncement. His name was Michael Hirst, and a photograph was therefore instantly taken and dispatched to him.

Buffy had to wait over a month before he heard back from Christie's. He made Martin promise to call him the moment Hirst had been to see the picture. Although Hirst received the photograph while in Italy, he was insistent on seeing the picture before commenting, and Buffy had therefore to try and forget the picture and to carry on life as normal until he was telephoned by Martin. But he had a sick feeling. He knew how things could go wrong at the final stage with scholars' attributions, and that however much empirical evidence is mustered, authentication also requires an open-minded academic with an objective and reliable eye. This cannot always be guaranteed. Generally, the standard of objective art-historical expertise is high in Britain, but it has occasionally been known for art historians to reject attributions if the new work does not fit into their published and perceived perception of the artist – even if this appears to fly in the face of common sense and clear visual evidence. It will also be recalled, from Chapter Two, how Dave Dallas had suffered three times in a row at the hands of art historians who changed their minds, and Buffy had also encountered similar problems in the past. The art world, however, in which he had chosen to earn his living, has appointed its own judges of quality control and however frail the system may seem, no major work of art can be sold until these arbiters have been deferred to. Furthermore,

Michael Hirst was known for his scrupulous academic objectivity, and could be trusted to give a sound response.

Buffy was at home when he received the call. He had been warned that Hirst was due that day and, having had a month to think about it, had prepared himself for the pronouncement by expecting the worst. He was too war-weary in the field of art dealing to predict victory until the last skirmish was over. As it was, his caution was unfounded. Hirst had been taken by Martin to the warehouse in Christie's basement, and shown the slate painting as it lay propped against the racks containing a thousand other pictures being catalogued for sale. As soon as he had left, Martin, as promised, went straight to a telephone. 'Michael Hirst has seen the picture and dates it to after the sack of Rome in circa 1532. He has described it as a hitherto unknown, and fully authentic, work by del Piombo. Well done.'

The same ocean of relief that had engulfed Buffy the moment he had bought the picture in Chester, did so again now. For less than two hundred pounds he had found a Renaissance masterpiece, by far the greatest purchase of his life, if not a lifetime, and all the evidence and academic judgement was now inescapably in its favour. Martin offered to place the picture in their next old-master sale in December with a full-page illustration. He had no specific proposals for the estimate at this stage, but suggested a provisional valuation of £500,000. Buffy was too soaked in the drama of the moment to discuss its future further on the telephone, but promised to get back to him before the sale deadline. He needed time to dry off.

There was no doubt that a sum of this size could substantially alter the quality of his life and business. But was now the right time to sell? The stock market had recently taken a fall, and the knock-on effects were already being felt. What if there were no ready buyers prepared to risk large sums in the market at this time? The picture might fail, and to do so publicly at auction could seriously damage its future. No one likes a failed picture, least of all dealers with the burden of later having to explain why to potential clients. Buffy tussled with the options for a couple of months and with the deadline for the Christmas old-master sale fast approaching, finally decided to risk it. He agreed with Martin that no estimate should be published in the catalogue, leaving the market free to establish its own perception of the picture's value – a technique the auction houses use for great works of art they do not wish to hobble with prejudged estimates. Too high, and the cost may deter some buyers, too small, and they might inhibit some purchasers from preparing sufficient funds in the event of heavy competition.

Three weeks before the auction Buffy received a catalogue, and for the first time saw his picture reinstated in its rightful splendour – an eight-inch-high colour illustration, facing a page of expert commentary written by the auction house. Most reassuring of all was the bold heading naming the artist unequivocally as 'Sebastiano Luciani, called Sebastiano del Piombo'. Beneath the text were the two ominous words reserved for the great and the expensive, in the place of the normal estimate: 'Refer Department'. It wasn't till then, Buffy recalls, that he fully appreciated the extent of the picture's quality and importance. Although the painting was still dirty, the colour illustration taken under photographer's lights had an effect similar to that of white spirit in revealing its colour and range of tones, together with hidden detail, much of which was lost to the eye in normal light. It had come a long way, he reflected, since its perfunctory and unillustrated sixteen-word description in the general sale in Chester six months earlier.

It was a cold December morning, and Buffy slipped unnoticed into the fug of a crowded auction room, ten minutes before his picture came up for sale. The throng was even greater than usual, with television cameras and journalists adding to the usual assembly of traders, auction staff, vendors and collectors. Almost without exception, every national newspaper had become alerted to the story, which had all the elements of a classic tale of discovered treasure, thanks to the cheapness of the Pope's purchase price. How the news had got out, Buffy did not know, and he was keen to keep a low profile – at least until he knew the picture's fate, by which time his thoughts would be clearer. The sale was not doing too well, prices had been patchy, with some lots failing to reach their reserve, but there was a palpable heightening of tension as the auctioneer neared Lot 163, the star of the sale. The whole European old-master trade appeared to be present, mostly besuited, either lodged in chairs talking with colleagues, or packed thickly in a standing crowd at the rear, spilling into the next room. At the opposite end of the room, next to the auctioneer's mahogany rostrum, sat a row of Christie's staff with telephones, waiting for, dialling or gently exhorting blind bidders, who could be anywhere from Mexico to the room next door. Above their heads was a large screen translating the prices into other currencies, flicking off and then on again with each strike of the gavel. When Lot 163 lit up, the background hum ceased and Buffy, hidden behind some Italian dealers in the corner, noticed 'an instant and deathly hush'. There was hardly a person in the room who did not know the recent history of the painting before them, and for the second time that year the Pope was under the gavel. This time the bidding started more optimistically at £250,000. At first there was no bid. Buffy heard some whispering near by and noticed, in the trauma of the moment, that a couple of dealers had spotted him and were busy pointing him out to others. Again the auctioneer called out for a quarter of a million, but the room remained silent. Buffy began to chew his lip in solitary anguish, and just as the auctioneer's passive features began to show a tremor of concern, one of the telephone bidders frantically waved from behind his counter, the bid was accepted, and the contest began.

The auctioneer referred to his book and came back with £260,000, returning either another bid, or, more likely, the undisclosed reserve. With only the auctioneer and one telephone bidder, the price then rose steadily by increments of £10,000. At £380,000 the auctioneer ceased to look down and instead cast his eyes across the room. There they remained, for there was now nothing left to push the telephone bidder any higher, and it was up to the assembly of collectors, dealers and other telephones to take it further. No bid was forthcoming. His face and declaration of 'I'm selling at three hundred and eighty thousand' attempted desperately to cajole a further offering, but the silence was resolute. After a remaining few seconds the gavel came down, and Buffy's picture was sold.

Buffy was pleased and disappointed in equal proportion. He had made over a third of a million pounds before tax and opportunities now presented themselves to improve his lifestyle and increase his business. Not long afterwards he bought his country house in Hampshire, and used some of the remaining proceeds to buy a share in a racehorse appropriately named del Piombo, which has since run with some success at Edinburgh and Pontefract. 'But I don't recommend it,' he comments with maudlin wisdom. 'They cost too much to run.' For the truth of the matter was that the painting could have made very much more. Perhaps partly because of the pre-publicity, which may have put off some buyers who would have begrudged spending a vast sum on something acquired by another so cheaply, and also because the art market was suffering from a dose of financial insecurity, the auction seemed lacking in competitive fever. There are also some who believe that had the estimate been published, indicating that the vendor would have been happy to accept under a million, more dealers would have chanced bids. The words 'Refer Department' led some to believe that the reserve was in excess of a million and therefore out of reach.

There was, however, a third and to my mind more obvious reason for the lacklustre price. In retrospect this was perhaps a painting Buffy should have decided to clean, for a number of the more serious art buyers and institutions were fazed by its condition. Rarely, if ever, presented with a picture on slate of this importance, they were concerned that its surface might not improve, that the particular paint used, the unorthodox and porous surface on which it was applied and the stubborn-looking discoloration might mean it was impervious to cleaning solvent. Some even felt that the Pope's neck was damaged beyond repair. Finally, it was two dealers, Agnew's in partnership with an American gallery, Newhouse, who were prepared to take the risk, partly on the advice of the restorer Sarah Walden. Although present in person at the sale, it was they who were the anonymous bidders on the telephone, and only they were prepared to take the gamble in the belief that the picture would clean better than the rest of the trade had forecast.

They were to be proved right. In their words it restored 'magnificently', and richly fulfilled its potential (*Fig. 20*). Adam Williams of the Newhouse Gallery in New York put it more bluntly: 'It was pitch black in 1987. We took a huge risk. If it [had] cleaned like a dog, you'd be dead.' All the colour hinted at by the white-spirit tests proved to be clear and sustained, and the character and quality that subsequently emerged allowed Agnew's to proclaim it as the prototype for others, 'incomparably the grandest and most assured' of del Piombo's portraits of Clement, and thereby elevated even higher in the ranks of Renaissance art. They turned the oddness of slate as a background into a unique selling-point, highlighting the advantages of the material as described by Vasari, the Renaissance art historian and artist, according to whom, slate 'pleased people greatly, for it appeared by this means pictures could be eternal and such that neither fire nor worms could harm them.'

Buffy became a celebrity overnight and journalists trekked to his door to gain the full story of the man they crudely dubbed 'the Hoover' because of his tendency to acquire huge quantities of canvas. Sotheby's contacted the Pope's previous owner, who to this day remains anonymous: 'we have been in frequent contact with our original vendor since this matter came to our notice,' they announced to the press, and settled out of court damages, which were thought to be for the full sale price of the picture. A photograph, it was claimed, had been sent by Sotheby's Chester branch to London for comment, and had been returned, duly described as a copy.

Where an obvious oversight, or seriously missed attribution, leads to substantial loss for a vendor, the auction house will sometimes offer compensation to avoid legal action or, equally, in order to maintain good public relations. The figure will be arrived at by discussion, there are no set guidelines, and the negotiations are normally initiated by the vendor who has come to hear about their sleeper's belated awakening. Negligent cataloguing and misattribution would also fall into the general category of risks covered by a comprehensive liability policy taken out by most professional organisations, including auctioneers. The full definition of negligence is discussed further in Chapter Seven.

From a dealer's perspective, however, it is easy to see how the small Polaroid snap of this dirty picture in the morning's post might have appeared distinctly unexciting, and these sort of oversights will continue to be made as long as there is an art market.

Wandering up Bond Street a few years later, Buffy Parker found himself outside Agnew's and summoned up courage to ask one of its directors, Christopher Kingzett, to show him the cleaned picture. He was taken to one of their damask-lined showrooms and it was revealed to him in its fully and splendidly unmasked form, rid of all the grime that had so diminished its presence in Chester in 1987. Buffy was amongst the last dealers in England to see it before it left for America and the Getty Foundation in 1991, where it now resides. Now further established as one of the more significant portraits of the High Renaissance, they were happy to pay the reported sum of £6.5 million to secure it for their collection of old-master pictures.

Buffy is still traversing Britain in search of art, and continues to acquire pictures at the same prodigious rate. Although he will always be remembered for the Chester del Piombo, in commercial art history he should really be fêted for proving, more clearly than anyone else, how indefatigability produces its just reward. From a sentimental point of view, it could be said that Buffy did not receive his full reward. But Buffy is a realist. Christie's had correctly attributed the del Piombo, and there was therefore obviously no grounds for compensation, as there had appeared to be for the original vendor at Sotheby's. It was the skill of the trade that capitalised on the sale of the Pope second time around, a trade in which Buffy, as a travelling dealer, plays an exemplary and tireless role, and in which he will continue to thrive doing exactly what Agnew's and Newhouse did with his picture, although not, perhaps, on so momentous a scale.

CHAPTER FOUR

Discovery by Detection

WILLIAM DRUMMOND looked anxious. He was standing in an upstairs room at the Tate Gallery in London, having just unwrapped a painting which two hours earlier he had transported on his scooter from Covent Garden. The fateful meeting had begun with lunch in the Whistler Restaurant below the main galleries – although he had hardly eaten a crumb – and he now stood back to allow his painting to be examined, the little landscape that had occupied so many of his waking hours for the last six months. This, he believed, was to be a lost painting's rediscovery, 165 years after it had been painted in a Suffolk field by the leading British landscapist, John Constable. It now lay before a man whose pronouncements on authenticity where Constable is concerned, are often accepted as all but final.

The man was Leslie Parris, a Keeper of the British Collection at the Tate, who has already appeared once in these pages as the expert to whom Debo Gage took the Constable sketch in Chapter Two. During his career he had seen countless would-be works by the artist, and was now quite used to, more often than not, politely and firmly turning them down.

Since his entry into the trade in 1957 Bill Drummond could not recall ever having prepared so comprehensive a brief – a written presentation that he had spent weeks putting together, and which he had already subjected to every possible objection. But he knew full well that one man's opinion, that of the man before him, could now dash it all in a second. Any art dealer would feel anxious in the circumstances: the shabby little landscape he had bought on a whim from the back of a van, his chance discovery of a clue in a remote Suffolk church, the days of trawling through libraries, archives, old correspondence, and art galleries, and the arduous preparation for this nerve-racking encounter with an authority on the artist. On a small scrap of paper which to this day he keeps carefully filed, he now recorded the opening of the final act in this drama by writing down the first eight words that came from Parris's lips as he angled himself forward for a closer look, words with which he had to agree as they summed up all too well the problems that had faced Bill in his arduous quest to discover the true identity of the picture: 'There is nothing like it for a start.'

Bill had been trading long enough in British pictures to know exactly what Parris meant. Now a private dealer with upstairs chambers in St James's, filled to overflowing like a don's study with drawings, objects, files and books, his long experience of handling choice British drawings and oil paintings has earned him an incomparable reputation for connoisseurship and diligence amongst his fellow dealers and academics.

William Drummond was born in 1934 in Purley near London, and although not from art-dealing stock (his father was a director of Pickfords, the haulage firm), he had been inspired when young by the proliferation of local junk shops, particularly around Dulwich where he lived and went to school. In these 'havens', as he describes them, he spent much of his time and almost all his pocket money. He made a particular acquaintance with a junk trader by the name of Mr Harradine, or 'Junky' to his friends, and spent many free hours rummaging through his stock. He then moved to Gloucestershire and 'Junky' was replaced by a new trader called Teddy Raymond who had once succeeded in buying a walled-up cellar of port in a house clearance. Bill would regularly join him for a glass, and a bag of chips, during his school lunch breaks. His early interest, like many children, was in daggers, guns and coins, but it was the fortuitous discovery of a high-quality 19th-century drawing of a soldier, which he bought for one shilling and sold for £4 to the Parker Gallery in London, that probably set his ambitions more directly towards art dealing. He was then fourteen years old. Exacting studies, as for many of today's art dealers, never really caught his imagination, and with the exception of art, architecture, and games, his schooling was not a success. His first headmaster wrote to his father, 'If your son doesn't improve I shall have to ask him to leave.' He didn't so he went. Bill remembers most fondly his education in Cheltenham, where he moved after Dulwich College. A sympathetic art master and inspiring school vicar, together with cycle rides to Tewkesbury and Gloucester, gave him a love and knowledge of Cotswold churches and architecture that has remained with him.

After his national service and a short stint in the City, Bill went to work for, and later became the partner of one of the leading British painting dealers, Sydney Sabin. It was during what he describes as these 'wonderful years' that he not only achieved a wide knowledge of British painting and drawing, but in the course of everyday dealing came into contact with, and by his natural charm endeared himself to, large swathes of the art world and the buying public. He was able to form relationships not only with the main art academics, but with international collectors such as Drue Heinz and particularly Paul Mellon. After eighteen years he parted from Sydney Sabin to start trading on his own – by now a highly regarded independent figure, with a large bank of contacts and potential clients. Although he opened his Covent Garden gallery with an overdraft, the future looked promising.

Bill Drummond's strategy for buying works is unclassifiable. He does not like to rely on the obvious places, such as major auctions and art sales, but instead waits for things to 'pop up', almost as if these inanimate objects willingly present themselves to him. Such was the case with the would-be Constable he was now showing to the Tate, and it had been the same with many other works before that. 'If you travel around enough,' he explains, 'things manifest themselves.' His early experiences in London junk shops have given him the adeptness of a truffle-pig at rooting out the desirable, and he unashamedly investigates any London skip he might pass: 'I am one of several West End dealers who is not proud to be seen looking into them. I even climb in,' he says, and is particularly pleased, during two heat-waves, to have found two electric fans in the same skip outside the London Library, the second two years after the first. Many of the works he publicly sells are physically small, sometimes extracted from portfolios in minor drawing sales or antique shops, to which he then adds his transforming expertise.

The oil sketch which he had carried to the Tate on the back of his moped on 2nd May 1980 had come from a source close to home. His elder brother Nicholas had till that time been more of a businessman and administrator than a dealer. A scholar and brilliant linguist, with a particular gift for obscure languages, he had made the leap from that world to exporting Impressionists to Japan, and had very recently decided to have a go at what his brother was up to. His pictures travelled around in the back of his Volkswagen van, which was more usually occupied by his wife, four children and a mass of animals.

He had showed Bill this small picture together with a few others. Neither brother could come up with a proper attribution to an artist, but Bill was greatly taken with the landscape, and asked to buy it. Nick was reluctant at first, but was persuaded to part with it when Bill pointed out that Brightwell, the subject of the painting, was not far from where his wife's family lived, near Sudbury in Suffolk. A few days later, Nick came up with a price of £150, and Bill became its new owner. It later emerged that Nick had purchased the picture from Bonhams, Lots Road, the less grand arm of the Knightsbridge auction house where they sell objects of lesser value, and where it had been catalogued as 'English School: View of Brightwell near Ipswich, oil on panel, unframed'. He had secured it with a bid of £38.

Bill was able to pick up the little picture in one hand, the size was 6 × 9 inches, and he now examined it closely. It was scruffy and dark, the discoloured varnish obscuring some of the tones and details, but the scene was clearly readable. It showed a typical East Anglian vista. In the foreground was a great earthen bank, behind which were a few buildings. Beyond them, a roadway wound its way into the distance towards woodlands and the sharp, square outline of a tiny church which punctuated the horizon. Walking towards it were two barely discernible human figures no more than a couple of millimetres high. In the top right-hand corner could be seen the side view of what appeared to be either formal barns or a middle-sized formal house. Turning it over in search of further clues (the automatic instinct of any dealer when presented with a picture for the first time), Bill then read the source for the catalogue description. A neat, ink inscription, or 'legend', that had become partly absorbed into the grain of the wood read 'Brightwell nr. Ipswich?'

Bill had enjoyed visits to East Anglia since childhood, and although he had no certain ideas about the possible artist, felt that the crisply defined little view beautifully evoked the familiar landscape; his nostalgic temperament caused him to fall for it instantly. He had no immediate thoughts of reselling it, and even considered presenting it to his wife's family, but decided in the meantime that he would enjoy it as his 'latest toy'. He propped it on a shelf in front of some books where it then stayed as another eyecatcher amidst the compelling clutter. Many months later he decided to have it cleaned, and so gave it to his restorer, together with a few other paintings, to do in her own time. Still undecided about the landscape's possible author, he was in no particular hurry, and experience had taught him not to pressurise a restorer unnecessarily: 'A good one is a treasure and not to be chivvied.' It is certainly true that the more popular restorers, often inundated by work, can sometimes react badly if you hurry them – as a doctor might if asked to speed up an operation – and there is a critical point when exhortations to return a picture are perceived as bullying intrusions. In this instance the restorer was given ample time, and in the meantime Bill's focus moved on to other things, making the little landscape's return, many months later, an even more welcome surprise. For it is true to say that he now owned a very different picture (*Fig. 21*).

Bill opened the waxed brown paper in which it was wrapped to reveal a transformed image. The grime had been removed, presenting him with a staggering mass of new delights, subtleties and details. Where there had been a dark, yellow-brown, subduing haze, there were now horses in a field, a flock of sheep and clusters of cornflowers along the path; the formerly muddy brown earthen bank had switched into a brilliant reddish slope of sand. 'Below it I could now even see ducks dabbling in a ford beside a small bridge,' he recalls with delight. Although the background of the scene was overcast, the pollarded willows and ripe cornfields were now lit up by pools of sunshine, and the two miniature figures had turned into brilliantly defined flecks of red and black. Bill was no nearer being able to identify the artist, but his little landscape had become mesmerising.

Throughout Christmas the image's enchantment remained with him, particularly as he found himself later in East Anglia, staying with his wife's parents near Sudbury. One particular afternoon, he and his wife Nina decided that they were in need of a healthy walk; unsurprisingly the choice of 'Brightwell near Ipswich' suggested itself.

It was no more than a dot on the map, probably the smallest village in Suffolk, with neither a shop nor a pub and consisting of little more than a small church, a handful of cottages and a population of around fifty. 'Where does one start in a place like this?' he asked himself. The church seemed the obvious place to go and, trying the door, he found it open. So small was the church that at one time it had been referred to as a chapel, but it was generously filled with substantial memorials and hatchments to local families, together with some gilded armour from the Barnardistons – the most prominent of these historic parishioners. It was getting dark, but by ferreting around Bill was able to find more traces of this old family who seemed to have either died out or moved away in the 18th century. Bill did not know what he was looking for – apart from the brief description on the back of his picture he had no firm leads – but like his forays around junk shops and skips, he left himself open to things manifesting themselves: his approach was to be receptive and unprejudiced – even the unlikely could be considered. He remembers that the air was still and cold; hugging his coat to him, he made his way slowly around the interior of the church, processing and retaining any useful information that came to him. Arriving back almost where he had started, on a corner wall next to the door, wrinkled and stained by damp, he then saw a large-scale early-18th-century print of a house (*Fig. 22*). Bill recognised it instantly as a typical work by Kip after Knyff – known to enthusiasts of old houses and garden schemes for his ambitious bird's-eye perspectives as if done from a balloon, many of which were published in a tome called *Britannia Illustrata* (1707). The print's condition suggested that it had been hanging there for many years, probably given by a parishioner to record what Bill now gathered was the vanished great mansion of

Brightwell Hall. Not only did it show the grand house itself but its surrounding land, consisting of plantations, avenues of trees, a fishing lake and, as a minor detail, some distance from the house, the church in which he was now standing. His eyes then moved to some nearby framed pages from an early-19th-century journal called the *Gentleman's Magazine*, a publication not dissimilar to the *Spectator* in its day, in which learned gentlemen wrote on all manner of antiquarian subjects. This particular contributor, one E. H. T. Barnwell, was writing in 1829 and gave a full account, in didactic antiquarian's prose, of the gravestones in the church, a description of a medieval Gothic font and also of the Kip print Bill had just been looking at. Most casual readers at this point would have lost interest after the first paragraph, but Bill, with an interest in church monuments developed while at school in Gloucestershire, read and absorbed every word with an enthusiast's stamina. Holding Bill's interest with his scholarly detail, the chronicler then mentioned as an almost casual aside, '. . . I have a watercolour drawing [of the house and its surroundings] copied from an oil painting by Mr Constable of Upper Charlotte Street, Fitzroy Square, in the possession of Sir Robert Harland . . .' This was buried in the last paragraph of the second column of dense print, and for a moment Bill thought his mind had fabricated it. He went back to the top of the paragraph, and read it again, this time more deliberately. Constable was not an artist he had considered as a contender for his picture's author, but could, just could the oil painting referred to here be his very own?

It would soon be dusk, but Bill and Nina hurriedly made their way out of the church and tried to find the site of the house. It seemed an obvious, although perhaps not fruitful next step, as Mr Barnwell had pointed out that the house had been pulled down in *c*.1730, and therefore a good seventy-five years before the likely date of Bill's picture. They marched at a strenuous pace to where the house seemed likely to have stood and found, as they suspected, that almost every trace of Brightwell Hall had vanished from the landscape. The only possible clues to its former existence were some substantial, well-designed stables and barns, which might have once been linked to the house, and which were set back from the road at the end of an avenue of ancient trees. Bill closed his eyes to recall the composition of his landscape, and managed to bring to mind a hazy recollection of something like these barns in the lower-right middle distance of the picture. In the deepening gloom, he next tried to locate where the artist would have stood, attempting to find a point from which a lane wound to the right with the church on the left, and these barns and stables in the opposite corner. After a few moments by car and more by foot they homed in on the most likely place, at the edge of a copse. Time, however, had taken a heavy toll. The lane was now a metalled road and on the left, where once stood the low thatched barn, was now a 20th-century red-brick house.

By backing into some undergrowth, Bill attempted to position himself on the very spot where the artist would have stood. But trees had sprung up and a thicket now obscured the view. Although it was midwinter and dark, he tried nevertheless to visualise the colour and movement with which the artist would have been presented on a glorious summer's day in Regency England: the blustery sky, occasionally releasing shards of sunlight on to the gentle slope; the wild flowers and cow parsley suggested by the flecks of white paint in the landscape's foreground; on the road in front of him, once a sandy lane, the occasional traffic of carts bumping along the track; and in the far distance two figures, in black and red, inching their way towards the church. He thought of the artist surveying his blocks of watercolour (for the oil would probably have been preceded by a watercolour sketch) and the feat of recording this orchestra of infinite natural tones, colours, and movement into a form worthy of its subject. Returning to the 20th century, and looking down at the tangle of foliage around his ankles, he then asked himself the question which, in varying forms, would return to him a thousand times over the next five months: 'Am I standing in the footprints of John Constable?'

Bill returned to London in the first week of January, and sat down at his desk with the little landscape propped before him, gazing at it with a new sense of intimacy. He wrote down his two new advances. Despite the question mark after the inscription, thanks to his trip he now knew for certain that this *was* a view of Brightwell. Also, according to Barnwell, who was writing his article in 1829 (and therefore during Constable's lifetime), there had existed a Constable oil painting of the scene, then in the collection of one Sir Robert Harland, and of which Barnwell had a watercolour copy. The date of the article increased the likely accuracy of this information. To look at, however, the painting did not immediately suggest Constable's style, and this was to be a problem that troubled him repeatedly over the next few months. The small-scale oil works of the artist, normally referred to as sketches, have a looseness, fluency and verve on which his modern reputation is largely founded. Although his large exhibition pieces such as 'The Hay Wain' and 'The Cornfield' reveal a mastery of handling and design, it is the smaller, more personal records of English landscape for which he is most highly regarded — the captured effects of light on trees, in water and behind clouds, nature on the move in all its multifarious guises and which he seizes with an unhesitating eye and brush. The little landscape had elements of this quality of observation, but seemed a little too ordered, too carefully arranged and constructed to evoke these characteristics and to many would suggest the work of an artist influenced by Constable (of which there were a great number in mid-19th-century England), rather than of the master himself. And yet it also possessed a freshness, a deftness, and an originality of interpretation which seemed just too good to be the work of a minor painter. To turn this hunch into substance, however, Bill needed more solid proof. He therefore decided to try and enlist the help of the *other* acknowledged expert on Constable, Ian Fleming-Williams.

Fleming-Williams had co-catalogued the 1976 Tate Gallery Constable exhibition, taking a particular interest in the chronology of the artist's works as disclosed by his correspondence and painted and written documentation. Bill knew him and had in fact been invited down to a 'Brains Trust' on careers at Charterhouse School with three other dealers – all old boys – when Fleming-Williams was art master there.

Although an acknowledged authority on the artist, Fleming-Williams also had the advantage of being an independent expert, not formally attached to the Tate Gallery. When it finally came to presenting his argument to the Establishment, Bill wanted to hit them with overwhelming impact. But if he involved the official arbiters themselves in his preparation, he reflected, he might lose the element of surprise, and his enquiries could work against him, appearing as doubts. But a Fleming-Williams was none the less a recognised and much respected art historian, and Bill did not want to risk going out on a limb. He therefore approached the matter cautiously and, taking pen to paper to wish Ian all the best for 1980, casually went on to ask if he knew of any drawings connected with Brightwell, revealing no more of his intentions than that. Four days later, on 15th January, he received the expert's neatly scripted reply.

After the initial courtesies, he went on to say that Constable was recorded as having been commissioned to paint a view of the scene by the author of the article in Brightwell church, the Reverend Mr Barnwell of Bury, in July 1815. He knew of the contribution to the *Gentleman's Magazine*, but was also able to cite correspondence from Constable on the commission, and added in the final paragraph, 'I know of the whereabouts of neither the oil (or any oil of Brightwell) or the watercolour; I wish I did. Please let me know if you discover either.'

Bill reacted excitedly – here were three new facts: Barnwell was the man who had commissioned the picture; it was known to be recorded by the artist himself; and furthermore the painting had not been found. The letter's contents urged him to drop everything and head straight for the London Library, where he knew he would find Constable's published correspondence. But before he did so, he penned a reply to Fleming-Williams, now informing him that he might well have the very same view in oil referred to, and in due course would be delighted to show it to him. But he exhorted him to keep it confidential for the time being. 'How very exciting,' Fleming-Williams wrote by return, asking to see the picture at the first available opportunity, and adding '. . . my lips are sealed'.

Bill sat cross-legged on the antique iron floor of the London Library in St James's Square, fired with the excitement of the chase, around him heaped every Constable book he could lay his hands on. He still had much work to do before he could think of announcing the picture, particularly in reconciling the land-scape's stylistic traits with those usually associated with the artist. At this juncture, however, he decided to channel his energies into producing a documentary case for its existence, gleaning as much evidence as he could on the commission, and its context within Constable's known works. His endeavours were therefore more to do with history than with art at this stage. He wanted the case to work on paper before he launched into the less prag-matic realm of stylistic analysis.

In a piecemeal form, extracted from the available biographies and art-history books, he began to re-create the circumstances in which the young artist found himself in the summer of 1815. This stage of the artist's life was later written up by Ian Fleming-Williams independently, but the following account is also some-thing Bill was now putting together from his own findings.

On 6th July Constable left London for a change of scene in East Bergholt, in Suffolk, which he regularly did in the summer

Fig. 19. *Pope Clement VII* before cleaning, as encountered at auction.

Fig. 20. The del Piombo *Pope Clement VII* cleaned. Collection of the J. Paul Getty Museum, Malibu, California.

Fig. 21. Brightwell(?) near Ipswich.
Fig. 22. Jan Kip after Leonard Knyff: the print of Barnardiston Hall.

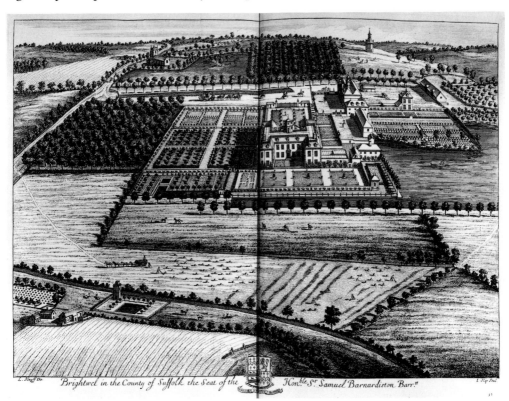

L. Knyff De.   *Brightwel in the County of Suffolk the Seat of the* Honble Sr Samuel Barnardiston Barrt.   I. Kip Seul.

Fig. 23. The portrait of *Prince Arthur* at auction.

Fig. 24. (*opposite, top left*) *Prince Arthur* (?) The Royal Collection, Her Majesty The Queen.

Fig. 25. (*opposite, top right*) A cleaning test showing the original Tudor green beneath later paint. Also visible is the edge of the right-hand wooden border of *Prince Arthur* at auction.

Fig. 26. (*opposite, bottom left*) X-ray of *Prince Arthur* showing its clipped upper edge and its original, niche-shaped format.

Fig. 27. (*opposite, bottom right*) *Prince Arthur* in mid-restoration with top and side additions removed.

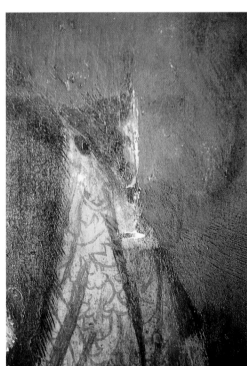
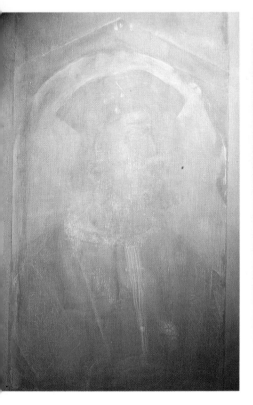

Fig. 28. *Prince Arthur* restored and in its new frame.

Fig. 29. *George Washington* at the New York auction.

Fig. 30. A dollar bill showing reproduction of the same portrait type.

Fig. 31. The picture at auction attributed to Guido Cagnacci.

Fig. 32. Antonio Canaletto: *The Grand Canal*, looking north east from the Palazzo Tiepolo towards the Rialto

months to replenish his artistic lifeblood and see his family. The weather was ideally suited to the painting and recording of the Suffolk landscape and his spirits were high. He was also in love, and wrote to his betrothed, a Suffolk girl by the name of Maria Bicknell, that the place 'never looked half so beautiful before as now'. Fleming-Williams has pointed out that Constable did not like to tell his future wife 'what he was about' and in his letter uninformatively reported to her that he was going to meet 'a gentleman [the Reverend Mr Barnwell of Bury] at a village [Brightwell] near Woodbridge to take a view for him of the church as it appears above a wood'. Fleming-Williams has also been able to organise some of the works that Bill was now seeing illustrated in the books about him into a narrative of part of the artist's progress. Dated drawings of Woodbridge (3rd August), Framlingham and Ipswich (5th August) show the route the artist took on his way home from Brightwell, and a letter from Barnwell, referred to by Constable, indicates that he was returning from a job well done: 'he [Barnwell] was most pleased with the little picture,' he was able to report with some satisfaction. There was further correspondence about a frame, in which Barnwell asked for a 'rich', 'handsome' one — but not as large as those dictated by the fashion of the day.

Although Bill trawled through the rest of the correspondence, together with all the literature relating to recorded drawings and oil paintings, plus the accounts of contemporaries, until his eyes hurt, he could find no further references to the commission. But as documentary evidence this was already far more than could be fairly expected. Serendipitously, in the course of his research he had also established two vital pieces of information that might help explain the painting's untypical style. He now knew that this was one of Constable's rare formal commissions, in other words it was paid for by a client who had demanded a specific view for his money of 'the church as it appears above the wood'. Much as a portrait painter is expected to record a likeness of the face in front of him, so Constable's natural picturesque leanings may have had to be constrained by the requirements of a client wanting a specific topographical record. Normally in landscapes of this small size, Constable would have been using his almost impressionistic, sketchy style with the purpose of recording essential atmospheric conditions and other physical information to employ in the composition of his larger, exhibited works. But not so for this one: Constable was painting to order. The fact that it was unusually small for a formal work is further indicated by Constable's reference to 'the little picture' in his own correspondence. In other words, even the artist thought it small! By the end of his documentary searches, Bill felt his case was strengthening.

The Tate Gallery and Victoria & Albert Museum hold more works by Constable than anywhere else in the world, and Bill's next step was to steep himself in the original drawings and paintings. He spent many hours sifting through boxes of drawings and watercolour sketches at the Victoria & Albert, and a further weekend with the oil paintings, applying himself with titanic zeal. He homed in on the small compositions, scrutinising the paint strokes, the way shadows were applied beneath trees, the flecky way in which the artist denotes flowers and cattle, and the foreground clumps of grass and stones; he fathomed his technique of using vibrant colours to express normally dull substances like sand or tiled roofs, and his trick of patterning landscape with shards of sunlight. He also spent many further hours in the Witt Library, poring over photographic reproductions of every known and attributed work in museums and private collections throughout the world, seeking anything that could give him more visual knowledge and better comparisons. By the end of the gargantuan trawl through all the main repositories of work, his head ringing with views of the Suffolk countryside, and details of the artist's life now lodged consciously, he began to feel as though he knew the traits of Constable as he would those of a long-standing friend.

He also was getting to the point where he knew that he had done everything reasonably in his power to elevate his little shelf ornament into a lost Constable. However, he had still found nothing that, stylistically, accorded closely with his own painting. This last stage would now have to be achieved by means of his own instinct. Bill now decided, confidently and conclusively, that although there was no clinching comparison, his painting *had* to be the work of Constable. He had scrutinised getting on for a thousand works by the artist, and felt he now knew the man. He also thought he knew the commission. Given his knowledge of both the painter and the subject, his little picture was exactly what he would have expected of Constable. So, even though the vital comparison that would convince the most stubborn sceptic might be missing, Bill made the leap.

As he attached his picture to his scooter on the momentous day of the appointment, together with the wedge of accumulated photostats, he realised that his own conviction, however unwavering, would count for little if Leslie Parris did not accept it. Ian Fleming-Williams had not yet seen the picture, but even if *he* accepted the work as by Constable and Parris did not, as a dealer he knew that a divided opinion amongst two of the main authorities can be as unhelpful to resale as outright rejection. Making his way across London in the dense traffic, he kept on asking himself the questions he might soon be faced with. He had not been able to find out who consigned the picture for sale, and there was a large unfilled gap in the provenance between Sir Robert Harland and himself. He had learnt that Harland had lived next to Brightwell, and that the land surrounding the church had belonged to his wife's family, the Vernons. When the main branch of the family died out in 1860, Harland's wife is said to have left what remained of the Vernon estates to a married niece of her husband's. But no more was known than that. A family link with the present day descendant who last owned the picture would have given Bill near conclusive proof of the painting's authenticity, but it was not forthcoming. Nor could he explain why Barnwell, the man who commissioned the oil painting, had only ended up with a watercolour copy; and he was unable to locate the watercolour, or establish the reason for the oil painting's transfer into Harland's collection. But these, he consoled himself, were just the question marks.

Bill also rehearsed a last line of defence should Parris, accepting the broken provenance, reject the painting on stylistic grounds. He remembered that the influential painter-diarist, Joseph Farrington, on 23rd July 1815, had reported Constable as saying that his landscapes were too 'unfinished', and that he should look at the works of the 17th-century romantic landscape painter, Claude Lorraine, for guidance. It is known that Constable actually did this before leaving London that year, and should the stylistic issue arise, it would be a further piece of justifying evidence for Bill to throw in: he could point out that the still impressionable artist was labouring under the influence of another, rendering his work untypical.

Bill knew Leslie Parris well enough to invite him for lunch before the hearing, together with Judy Egerton, another member of the Tate's staff. By the time the trio repaired upstairs for the viewing after lunch, they had hardly yet broached the purpose of his visit. Bill unwrapped the unframed picture and stepped back to allow the painting to work its magic. Parris at first said nothing, half-closing his eyes and scrutinising the painting carefully. 'There is nothing like it, for a start,' he said, and then picked it up and turned it over, reading the inscription that had already taken Bill to the remote hamlet in Suffolk. Concentrating with fixed intensity, he then placed the painting back on the table, maintaining a silence that began to go into its second minute. Bill could bear it no longer. 'What do you feel?' he asked. Parris smiled and turned slowly towards him. 'We could do with a Constable like this in our collection.'

After the indecision that every dealer suffers when given the opportunity to sell for a small fortune a picture that he has managed to buy, relatively speaking, for nothing (an indecision that normally only lasts a few minutes, particularly when, like Bill, you have an overdraft to pay off) Bill negotiated the sale of the painting to the Tate for £100,000. When Ian Fleming-Williams finally saw it, he readily agreed to its authenticity, and described it as 'a little descriptive masterpiece'. It was widely regarded as an exceptional work by the artist, highlighting a less known aspect of his oeuvre. Notable also for its richly documented early history, the £37 lot made national television news, with articles appearing in both the popular press and learned magazines as far away as Caracas and New Zealand.

As a result of the media splash, Bill was telephoned by a man who owned a small watercolour sketch by Constable of the same view, and he duly went to see it. The watercolour was a similar composition to 'Brightwell Nr Ipswich?', and a label on the reverse explained that it had been done by Constable, at about the same time as the painting, and that the artist had given it to a small child whose father ran the smithy just seen behind the sandy bank on the right. The child had been watching Constable paint. Microscopic though they might appear, the figures making their way from the vicarage towards the church, one in black, the other in red and white, were identified on the label as Constable's client, the Reverend Barnwell, and the blacksmith's child. It was a thrillingly unexpected last revelation, giving Bill cause to point out that they must be amongst the smallest identifiable portraits in British art – a little over one millimetre high!

And what of Bill's brother who sold the picture on for a paltry £150? For a short while he was mobbed mercilessly by some friends – including one who rang him in a foreign accent asking him whether he had any more Constables for sale. But after the excitement died down, and over the succeeding years, his brother has 'made it up to him in various ways,' I am clearly informed, 'in the course of subsequent art-dealing transactions between the two of them.'

Before the publicity broke, Bill managed to trace the family who had consigned the picture for sale to Bonhams. They were Quakers, long established in East Anglia, then living in Colchester, and Bill and Nina went to visit them at their home. Over tea, they told Bill how, moving to a smaller house, they had called in Sotheby's, who had selected various items to sell but discarded the picture as of no sale value. Bonhams followed in Sotheby's footsteps, had taken a similar view, but were prepared to accept the painting as a minor object for their Lots Road saleroom. They could not work out when the painting had entered into their family's possession, but many generations ago they had been Constable's bankers, and it may well have come to them around that time.

'I was surprised by how calm and amused they were, showing no bad sentiment,' Bill recalls. Some time later, however, after the publicity had died down, Bill was asked by their solicitor for his comments on whether there was a case against the two auction houses for negligence. In reply, Bill pointed out that as the picture was so untypical of a work by Constable, and in no way related to what is termed 'the received image of the master' they could be entirely forgiven, and that definitely no case ought to be brought against them: after all, even Bill, an established connoisseur of British landscape painters, had failed to realise its true authorship until his chance discovery in the Brightwell church set the trail in progress.

After tea, as Bill and Nina were leaving, one of the family called out, 'Goodbye, Mr Constable.' As they wound their way across country towards the London road, it struck Bill forcefully just how much of the young artist's soul he had absorbed over the last six months.

CHAPTER FIVE

The Specialist

PIERS PICKED OUT a catalogue from the pile in front of us and showed me a small painting on offer at a forthcoming London auction. Piers Davies had joined me nine months earlier for some brief work experience when he left Manchester University, and as I write this just over three years later, he is still here. His job is research. Each morning, from home and abroad, we receive an avalanche of catalogues, photographs and written details from auction houses, private owners and dealers. Part of his job is to survey these for objects to which we can bring transforming expertise. If something with potential is spotted, the next stage may then take him to art libraries, record offices, civil and mili-tary archives, guildhalls or a score of other repositories of infor-mation. What is found next could turn an unclassifiable curiosity into a compelling commercial artefact.

Our subject is British historical portraiture, but as dealers who have chosen to concentrate on one particular subject, we are far from alone. Art dealing in Britain has changed considerably over the last thirty years. Once, a small number of West End and country dealers handled virtually every antique picture of quality which came on to the market. In recent years, however, the market has become a very different place.

During the 1960s and '70s a rapid expansion in the world's economy, increased leisure time and better education produced a huge range of new collectors. There was more money with which to buy, more time in which to do it, and an increasing understanding of what to look for. Broadcasters such as Arthur Negus in *Going for a Song* heightened the public's fascination and lust for discovery, and this continues to be expertly exploited in *The Antiques Roadshow*. The market was bombarded with books on collecting and antiques, universities and museums offered accessible fine-art courses and saleroom reports began to feature conspicuously in the newspapers. It happened across the spectrum of art and antiques. Items that had once had little sale value, such as Victorian paintings, classic cars or turn-of-the-century ceramics, became collectable and acquired a following of their own. The auction houses, who act as agents for sellers and therefore do not need to buy the goods they sell, realised that, with the aid of publicity and marketing, they could bypass the dealer and reach the private buyers and sellers themselves. The new collectors accepted the invitation, and the auction houses, who once only supplied dealers and the occasional knowledgeable collector, began to turn into enormous international businesses with turnover and profits to match. They now have departments for almost every main area of collecting, and thousands of objects pass through their hands every week. Last year alone, for example, Christie's sold 217,245 lots in their salerooms around the world.

To compete in this changed market, many of the old firms, who once dealt in everything from 19th-century prints to Renaissance pictures, together with some of the newer galleries, became more specialist traders, developing specific areas of expertise. The auction rooms cannot always match such expertise, largely because of the tyranny of sales deadlines, and the sheer range of works they are required to handle.

There are notable exceptions to the specialist tendency, such as the Richard Green empire, three West End galleries which strive strenuously and successfully to offer only the very best art from across the fullest possible range. Some of the older firms, such as Agnew's, have retained their omnivorous interests and can also often resell pictures sold to clients half a century before. There are also single notables like Rafael Valls, whose discerning eye will consider almost any pre-1850 painting of high quality, or Colnaghi's, who have kept up their reputation for old-master drawings as well as paintings. The overwhelming trend, however, as I have witnessed it over fifteen years of dealing, has been for dealers to conquer a containable area, accumulating a group of loyal clients, a specific store of knowledge, and a skill and expertise with which the auction rooms, and other dealers, are not always able to compete on equal terms. For those who take their specialisation seriously, discoveries arise naturally, and provide essential compensation for the narrowness of the field.

The picture Piers showed me that morning was of an earnest-looking young boy, wearing a black cap and a gold robe, which had been put up for sale by the heirs of a British nobleman. It was illustrated prominently in colour on its own page – typical, in fact, of the sort of work which, as specialists in portraiture, we would give a second look (*Fig. 23*). The boy's body was sharply cut off by a shelf at its base, from which emerged two rather clumsy hands, like the paws of a hamster. In one he held what looked like a seeded dandelion. Appraising the painting with a jaundiced art-dealer's eye, it appeared to be in poor condition, the brushwork primitive and the proportions and anatomy unsatisfactory. The area around the subject's body was too expansive, and his shoulders and elbows too pronounced. But it was not all bad. The facial features were sensitive, seeming to convey a real individual, and at the risk of reading too much into it from a 20th-century perspective, he had an engaging look of wistful solemnity. The painting was described as 'English School, 16th Century; Portrait of Arthur, Prince of Wales (1486–1502); Head and shoulders, wearing robes and holding a rose; Oil on panel; 14¼ by 11¾ inches.' The artist, as is often the case with 16th-century British works, was unknown, and for a picture of this date, size and quality the estimate of £4,000–£6,000 did not seem out of order.

'I find this difficult to believe,' said Piers, 'but I can't find any other portraits of the Prince listed.' Ridiculous, I thought, he must have overlooked them. A royal child of this significance was bound to be represented, probably more than once, in our national institutions. For significant he was. Prince Arthur was the first-born of Henry VII and Elizabeth of York, heir to the newly established Tudor crown, and consequently a major focus of interest in his day. Arthur was born prematurely, was frail and weak thereafter, and at the age of eleven stood a foot shorter than his younger brother, Henry. Nevertheless he was arduously groomed for kingship from the start and strategically married off to Catherine of Aragon, daughter of Ferdinand and Isabella of Spain, the richest and most prominent ruling couple in western Europe. As befitted the Prince of Wales, after they married King Henry sent him to occupy the seat of his principality at Ludlow Castle, in the Welsh Marches. But shortly after the couple arrived in Ludlow, Arthur contracted a relatively mild form of the plague called the 'sweating sickness', and at the pitifully young age of fifteen died. The King and Queen, although distraught, quickly switched their attention to his younger brother, Henry, later Henry VIII, who was obliged to marry his brother's widow to safeguard the diplomatic and monetary advantages Arthur had won by the marriage. Later, using the excuse that his brother had already consummated the marriage with his young bride, an almost certain fabrication that he hoped would render his own union with Catherine incestuous in the eyes of the medieval church (who viewed a brother's wife as the same as a sister),

Henry subsequently divorced Catherine to marry Anne Boleyn. The Pope did *not* accept the situation, and as every schoolchild has been taught, this led to England's break with Rome and the Reformation. So although Arthur was himself a relatively unknown figure in English history, and had died as a young teenager, what he represented was of great significance, and if, *just if*, this were his only portrait, we would be dealing with a painting of great historical and commercial value.

Yet I was not holding my breath. We possess a comprehensive library on English and British iconography, collected haphazardly over the last ten years, and although far from exhaustive, through it I felt sure that we could quickly establish the existence of other portraits of Arthur. Kneeling before the larger reference books on the lower shelves, Piers and I then embarked on a task which, unknown to me then, would consume us over the next three weeks with the intensity of a burning quest: the hunt for the only true image of Arthur, Prince of Wales.

We first attempted to establish whether there were any portraits of him in the main National collections of England, Ireland, Scotland and Wales. We would also need to look to America, but that could not be done from our own library. As Arthur had married a Spaniard, we could not discount Spain either. Britain and Ireland were relatively easy, and we carefully checked all the exhibits in the National Galleries in Dublin, Edinburgh and London, for which we hold illustrated catalogues and can flip quickly through the indexes. Sometimes, though, revisionist cataloguing or recent acquisitions mean that these are out of date, and this necessitated telephone calls to the appropriate registrars. The process took a couple of hours, and despite a thorough survey of these, and other possible locations, Arthur was not to be found. For so important a figure, it amazed me that there seemed to be nothing. I also began to feel the first faint tinglings of opportunity.

America and Spain were a little more tricky. In the early

afternoon I rang the Smithsonian Institution in Washington, which incorporates the American National Portrait Gallery, and was connected to their archives and a woman sitting before a computer.

'Arthur who?'

'Arthur, Prince of Wales, heir to the Tudor throne,' I replied. Slightly fazed, she said she would be happy to feed in Arthur and try and establish whether he was recorded anywhere in the United States, but did not promise much joy. A minute later, having scrutinized the computer files, she returned with the information that there were no recorded portraits of Arthur in any museums or surveyed private collections throughout America. I could have 19th-century renderings of King Arthur of the Round Table if I wanted, and even cartoons, but from east to west, north to south, she was unable to find an original portrait of the young prince anywhere.

Spain was next. I rang a friend who had worked in the archives of the Prado in Madrid, a researcher turned dealer, and asked if he would make the necessary enquiries. He had had similar requests from me in the past, but could not help but be roused to interest when I added, 'and then forget I even asked you'. The auction was three weeks away, the picture was fully illustrated for all to see and, indeed, correctly identified. I did not want to turn it into a subject for general conversation.

In the meantime Piers had the task of tackling the British Museum. Our mounting spirits were then extinguished, albeit temporarily, when he was told on the telephone by a librarian in the Drawings Department that they possessed an illuminated manuscript portrait of Arthur. 'I knew it was too good to be true,' he said, and gloomily set off for the London Library a few hundred yards away in St James's Square, where he had been told there was a book that contained a reproduction of this portrait. An hour later he returned, his face brighter. The picture had been painted by a Bruges artist in the 1490s, and drew on a stylistic tradition that valued lively characterisation over accurate likeness; in other words, a tradition of facial and bodily 'types', rather than true portraits. In the manuscript Arthur was portrayed in two miniature portraits as an animated young prince, as befitted his contemporaries' expectations, but contrasting starkly with the sickly, diminutive child that history reports. We could therefore discount these contenders.

The most obvious place to look for other images of Arthur had yet to be investigated: the Royal Collection. The sumptuous collection of portraits and other works of art amassed by Charles I, as well as by his forebears and successors, is probably the finest in private ownership, and its contents are admired and studied by art historians across the globe. Although missing many of its original items, palmed off by Cromwell to creditors in lieu of payment in the new regime, a proportion were clawed back after the Restoration, including many of the early English works. The portraits of English monarchs are one of the Collection's strengths, naturally enough, the quality of which was hugely enriched by major painters of European renown such as Holbein and Van Dyck, who were lured by an English court hungry to be painted. Portrait-painting was a relatively new fashion in England which did not begin to take hold until the 1520s and 1530s and therefore anything dating from around 1500 or earlier, roughly Arthur's date, is extremely scant in England. I was not expecting a cavalcade of offerings – particularly as no royal portrait of Arthur had been included or referred to in any of the general Tudor history books we had trawled. It was then my turn for a setback when I was told by an assistant that the Royal Collection did indeed have a portrait of Arthur, and that it was housed at Windsor Castle.

'A real portrait of Arthur?' I asked. 'An original one done during his lifetime?'

'Yes,' they replied. 'Funnily enough, someone was asking us the very same question about a week ago.'

I needed a few seconds to take this in. Why the hell had I not started with the Royal Collection? It now seemed so obvious. Okay, I thought, so we were no longer dealing with a unique image. That was disappointing, but if the picture in the sale were 16th-century, as an early image it was probably still worth buying. Furthermore, at least now we had a portrait with which to compare it. For it had begun to occur to me that without any comparative facial proof we might never prove that the picture at auction was genuinely of Arthur anyway.

But who had been asking about it a week ago? At this stage, it was not much more than vanity on my part, but it irritated me that someone might have been thinking as we were, and had possibly stolen a march on us.

Although we keep all the published volumes of the Royal Collection catalogue, the particular pair that dealt with the 16th century, published in 1963, had been lent to a friend, which was one of the reasons why we had been obliged to telephone the Collection. Piers retrieved one of the volumes the following morning, and we placed the auction image next to the catalogue picture of the Royal Collection Arthur (*Fig. 24*). Scrutinising the two faces it then instantly hit us both that we were not looking at the same sitter. Stronger, broader and older, the royal portrait looked different from the soulful boy now up for auction. Furthermore, it could hardly show Arthur as a much older child, because he had died at fifteen, and the picture at auction showed a youth already bordering on adolescence. The sitter in the royal portrait also looked to be in his late teens or even early twenties and seemed most likely to portray a young Henry VIII, admired in youth for his handsome, athletic demeanour. I then noticed to my delight a question mark after the title 'Prince Arthur'. In other words, the compiler of the catalogue, Sir Oliver Millar, had doubted the identity also. Excitement and adrenalin flooded back, and the chase resumed.

Piers made an appointment with the Royal Collection library, and headed off to one of its administrative nerve centres – the library on the top floor of Stable Yard House in St James's Palace. The royal inventories were obviously the next place to look and from them we might be able to establish why and how the painting now hanging at Windsor had come to be called a portrait of Arthur, and indeed why this identification had been questioned. I was now gambling that this doubt, whatever form it took, would allow a different and more authentic image to supersede it. From experience, however, I knew it would not be easy as we were about to enter an academic labyrinth. In the lull that preceded the second phase of the search for Arthur, although barely audible, I could also now hear the unnerving tread of a second interested party. Who had telephoned the Royal Collection to ask about Arthur a week before we had? And had they given up, as we nearly had, when they heard of the other – different – image of the Prince? While reflecting on this, I received a call from the friend who had made the Spanish enquiries for me with the news that there was no sign of Prince Arthur in Spain, in either public or (recorded) private collections. Did I want to tell him what it was all about? 'Not quite yet,' I replied, but promised him an explanatory lunch – a week after the sale.

The royal library, Piers recalls, was steeped in silence. At one end of the room sat Christopher Lloyd, Surveyor of the Queen's Pictures, and in front of him, at desks placed at regular intervals down the room, were staff, assistants and researchers. Piers sat at one of these desks and before him were laid the leatherbound inventories of the Collection, ranging in size from folio to octavo. Likening the feeling of trepidation to sitting down to an examination, he then nervously opened the first, dated 1542. It had been compiled during the reign of Arthur's brother, Henry, and Piers was instantly faced with a stream of barely legible, spidery script. Gradually accustoming himself to the style, and running his eye down the contents, scanning for the name Arthur, he was soon rewarded with what appeared to be two references. The first clearly described the picture currently in the Royal Collection, mentioning that the subject was wearing a chain of red and white roses. The second was less explicit: 'Item oone [one] table [panel] with the picture of Prince Aurthure'.

The Royal Collection portrait then appeared again in another inventory, this time in 1637, and with a new identity. This inventory had been compiled by Charles I's loyal but harassed custodian of art, Abraham Van der Doort, who had hanged himself in 1640 when unable to find a misplaced miniature. Clearly a meticulous man, he had seen fit to change the identity of the portrait into that of Arthur's brother, Henry VIII, which would have fitted better with the older, more robust appearance of the subject. The description tallied so exactly that there could be no doubt it was the same one that had been named as Arthur in the 1542 inventory. Moving on to the next volumes, Piers then found the Royal Collection portrait listed in another inventory, this time after the Restoration, when it had been reacquired by the Royal Family after Cromwell's sell-off. But its identity had now been altered to Henry VII – its third transformation in the course of just over one hundred years. This alternating label – from Arthur, to Henry and then to their father – was therefore the reason, or a contributing one, for the painting's doubted identity as Arthur today.

Piers then reached again for Van der Doort's inventory of 1637, to see whether the *other* panel portrait of Arthur, mentioned but not described in the Tudor listing of 1542, also came up here. He then encountered a detailed description that nearly blasted him off his chair:

A Whithall   Item the i5th being Princ Arthure in his minoritye
peece   In a black capp and goulden habbitt houlding in
              his right hand a white gillifloore in a reed *pintit*
              goulden frame.

Apart from the size, which was given as 11 × 7 inches, this described exactly the portrait of the young prince at auction. What we had assumed to be a seeded dandelion, and the auctioneer had called a rose, was in fact a gillyflower – a 16th-century name for a wild carnation or pink, and a symbol of purity and royalty.

Piers then went looking through later inventories and soon found further references to what appeared to be the same portrait. But when he came to an early 18th-century listing of paintings in the collection, references to the picture ceased. It appeared that the picture had then vanished from the collection.

Charged with the excitement of the quest, Piers returned with his newly found evidence. There could be no doubt now that the picture at auction *was* Arthur – at least according to Van der Doort: thrillingly, it fitted the description exactly, with the exception of the 'reed *pintit* goulden frame' (red painted golden frame) and the dimensions (the auction picture was approximately 14 × 12 inches, and therefore over twice the span). As Piers recounted his findings, for a fleeting moment I hoped that this could be the same picture without its frame. But reflecting on the discrepancy in the size of the two pictures, this seemed impossible. It could, however, be an enlarged copy from the same period and, as a unique and possibly contemporary image, highly desirable.

I started to jot down the main points of progress. By the end of a heady week, we had established that there was no firmly accepted portrait of Arthur in existence in a public collection. We now knew that, except in size, the picture at auction fitted the exact description of one that had once resided in the Royal Palaces. The present Royal Collection portrait had emerged as a 'pretender' – doubted throughout the centuries, in the Royal Collection catalogue, and independently by ourselves. It was now time to go and see the picture at auction and convince ourselves that it was at least 16th-century, as catalogued, and therefore, crucially, contemporary to Arthur himself. A late copy would be of much less historical and commercial importance. Ideally, we also wanted to find further corroboration that the picture really was Arthur, and not a portrait which Van der Doort had mistakenly latched on to as a portrayal of the young prince. But this was an added luxury on which we could not count.

The sale was six days away, and the lots were not yet on view. Before pictures are hung in the main London auction rooms they are normally stored in the bowels of the building within an enormous subterranean maze of racks, shelves, and vaults of such complexity that a home-bound ant would lose its way. Only a few porters seem to hold the key to the underlying logic of the system. Together with those works about to be sold, the storage system also incorporates pictures that are uncatalogued, already sold, or 'bought in' and soon to be re-entered. It is a sublime feat of administration, and bewildered departmental experts have been known to find themselves humbled, and at the mercy of sometimes ruthless 'guardian' porters, to whom they must first put their case before an item is located.

We made an appointment for two days ahead. On Wednesday afternoon we entered the building by the back door. An assistant from the department then took us to the lift shaft, and from there down into the deep. A benign overalled porter guided us on the final leg to a makeshift easel in the middle of one of the largest rooms, bordered on all sides by hundreds of framed canvases in racks, the biggest works, over five feet high or more, propped against the walls.

Sitting upon the easel, looking diminutive and alone, we then came upon the now familiar form of Arthur. Fascinated to now encounter 'it in the flesh', I walked over and picked it up. The surface area of the little panel was no larger than a school exercise book, and it weighed about the same as a table-mat. The department had already taken it out of its later, 18th-century frame, thereby giving us unhampered access to the panel's physical condition, and we began our inspection.

A bottle of white spirit and an electric hand lamp stood ready for us. Plugging in the lamp and holding it a foot from the panel, we then scrutinised the painting's surface. At first sight the paint appeared alarmingly smooth, particularly in the background, and showed none of the signs of cracking or deterioration usually to be found in Tudor and Elizabethan paintings. In fact, it looked largely 18th-century – a good two hundred years later. But on closer inspection the face looked earlier. Although covered with a later transparent glaze of pink paint to make the complexion appear healthier, through the glaze I could detect a hard and creamy layer of original paint, broken up into a mosaic of *craquelure*. This looked like hearteningly aged Tudor paint, and it pushed the dating of this part of the picture back to the 16th century, and the period of British art as it emerged from the Middle Ages.

But the later paint worried me. It seemed to be covering a large proportion of the picture, particularly in the background, and now I could detect it in the robes as well. It would take a highly skilled restorer to remove it without damaging the layer beneath. But experience had told me that if the original paint was tough enough, and the added pigment permeable enough, the operation could be performed with solvents, and then if necessary scalpels. Assuming it could be done, it still left the question of why it had been covered over in the first place. The face was understandable – a cosmetic touch-up job of 18th-century 'foundation cream' which I had seen before on 16th-century portraits to remedy earlier white pallor. But why on the rest of the picture? Was it irrevocably damaged beneath? I asked for the white spirit and cotton wool, and applied a swab to the top half of the picture.

Achieving the familiar temporary effect, the background of 18th-century blue instantly shone, and the face of Prince Arthur lit up as if the sun had caught it, showing even more clearly the pale Tudor flesh hiding beneath its cosmetic hue. I did the same with the lower half. The gold robes showed up muddied by later paint, but Arthur's red and gold tunic resonated with a deep and ancient-looking lustre, suggesting pristine original paint. Within seconds the white spirit began to evaporate and the disguised but exquisite object, like a fading apparition, backed off into matt gloom. But Piers and I had both seen it, the memory was imprinted, and it burned fiercely over the next week.

A curious phenomenon then took place. Although the white spirit had now evaporated off the face and body, it still remained around the borders. This seemed to indicate that the consistency of paint in those areas was somehow different, or less absorbent. Here too it began to evaporate shortly afterwards, but remained long enough to give the fleeting impression that Arthur's body was placed in a sort of alcove, or compressed in some way. In the few seconds allowed, I was able to make out divisions running from the top to the bottom of the panel and through Arthur's shoulders. It seemed, in fact, as though borders had been added on to the main body of the panel, and I could now see that an attempt had been made to disguise the joints with what appeared to be even later paint. These borders had reacted differently to the centre of the picture when the spirit had been applied, suggesting a different type of wood or primer beneath. Turning it over, any further diagnosis was then foiled. The panel was covered with strips of canvas that concealed the back so completely that nothing more was deducible. I then asked for a tape measure and measured the width between these two apparent borders on the painted side. It came to approximately seven inches.

The realisation occurred to us both at once: that was the width of the lost royal image. It was only one dimension, however, and there were no signs of joinery at the top and bottom to indicate additions there also. But who knew what lay beneath the later paint? And if we could remove the canvas backing would we see signs of other changes? The possibility now presented itself that this could be the very painting which, in 1637, the meticulous Mr Van der Doort had measured for his master. And it is on occasions like this – in the early stages of a possible revelation – that the thrill of buying and selling pictures has no equal. The auction house had correctly identified both this picture's identity and date. It was now up to us, as specialists in our own territory, to take it the critical stage further.

Feeling it inappropriate to express our excitement there and then, we hurriedly left for the gallery to assimilate this latest development in private. As we were leaving the building I asked the assistant for a photograph of the picture (the auction houses normally have a few of each illustrated lot to hand out to potential clients). 'I'm sorry,' she replied, 'I gave the last one away to someone who was looking at the portrait this morning. I'll order some more, they'll be ready in a few days.' Convention and confidentiality forbid discussions about other clients, so I did not bother to ask her. But I shivered. We were being shadowed, I thought. This was the second time that I had come to hear of someone else on the trail of Arthur, and it left me feeling distinctly uneasy.

As we walked down Bond Street at a hurried pace, passing the large antique and art emporiums of Green, Mallets and Partridge's and the fashion houses of Gucci, Hermès and Versace, it occurred to me how the market for luxury never seems to fade. Even a subject as obscure as my own – historical British iconography – both suffers and benefits from acquisitive ardour. I caught sight of an affluent Arab alighting from a large Bentley to enter Asprey's on a buying trip, followed by a clutch of female companions in purdah masks. Across the road a member of the paparazzi, who has been wandering up and down Bond Street almost every day for as long as I can remember, was lining up his camera on a pop star's wife as she left Tiffany's. This is a street where people come to buy, sometimes objects of great value, I reflected. I am on the other side, not the buyer but the seller, supplying the demand. For once, I thought, I could reverse the roles. Why did I not try and buy Arthur against all competitors? Not as an item to sell, but as one to take home, like all those other shoppers. Perhaps it was the scent of competition, the lurking presence of an unknown rival, but as I neared the gallery this idea was turning into rock-solid resolve. The sentimental side of my nature had also taken hold. I was touched by the human drama: this could be the re-emergence of a lost child. Not only did it now appear to be the only facial record of Arthur, but possibly the official record of his likeness, the image by which Catherine of Aragon and others of the court would have remembered the deceased prince. It seemed a cruel hardship of fate that the heir to the Tudor throne – a child who provided the focus of so much expectation, and acted as such a vital pawn in a game he may only barely have understood – should have been blotted from the visual record of history. He had also died without his parents, and with a bride with whom he was too young to consummate his marriage, in a damp, cold castle, hundreds of miles from home in the Welsh Marches.

By the time we arrived at the gallery I realised that I had done something a dealer should never do with a prospective purchase. I had become attached. The memory of that apparition was working hard.

There were now five days to go, but this was Friday afternoon, the sale was on Wednesday morning and that left only two full working days to finalise our research. Looking at the catalogue illustration with fresh eyes, Arthur's robes now looked as though they had been widened, giving them the appearance of a cowl. It appeared that both the size of the body and the panel had been increased to turn it into a larger picture with greater impact. Early portraits, particularly of this date, were generally much smaller than those produced in subsequent centuries, and the enlarging may well have been done for reasons of fashion – or perhaps to make its size consistent with other panels in a larger set of later royal images. The implication was also that what I had feared was over-paint, possibly covering a damaged original layer, was for the most part later paint covering these additions. If we were correct, by removing the additions altogether, and assuming we could safely remove the paint that had been extended on to the background – done, no doubt, to blend and match the colour of the additional panels – we would only be left with the problem of the face, and the partly over-painted inner sleeves and cuffs. If this next stage of surgery was successful we could then return the painting to the compressed, jewel-like appearance typical of late 15th- and early-16th-century European portraiture. Extremely occasionally, such portraits were also to be found in England. Furthermore, if it transpired that there were additions to the top and bottom also, we would almost certainly be looking at the lost royal image. The combined uncertainty and excitement now made me feel queasy. I was desperate for the sale to be over and the issues of ownership, and the picture's own enigmatic state, to be decided.

We could still, however, work harder on lateral research. I asked Piers to look again into the provenance. We knew that the painting had come from the Earl of Granard – a Northern Irish family elevated in the 17th century – and I asked him to look again at the family tree, this time for any marriages to royalty, courtiers, servants, or indeed anybody who could have had a link with the royal palaces and their collections. If we could prove how it left the Royal Collection, the case for the portrait's being the lost royal image would be greatly strengthened. The present descendants had been selling a quantity of objects at auction, particularly books, and it was possible that some of these other items might have thrown up links with royalty.

As often happens at the eleventh hour, we then made a critical informational advance. A week earlier, Piers had found a casual reference to a picture of Arthur in the collection of the Duke of Northumberland at Syon House, near London. It had not been considered an authentic image by 19th-century scholars, and as we had encountered a number of later images of Arthur painted from imagination, including one in an early-Victorian mural in the Palace of Westminster, we had assumed it was just another of these. We had none the less ordered a photograph from the estate office — more than anything else to keep on file as a discounted claimant. The picture that arrived in the post was a tumultuous revelation.

It was a late-Elizabethan copy (c.1600) of the picture at auction! Painted on panel, and considerably larger, it was a typical 'corridor portrait' of the period, one from a set of Kings and Queens that frequently lined the long galleries and libraries of Elizabethan and Jacobean houses. Crude and simplified, as is typical of this genre of image, the artist had also misread the gillyflower for a seeded dandelion and placed the string of Arthur's pendant beneath the bodice, or outer tunic. But that it had derived from the picture at auction, or an identical source, there could be no doubt. There were also two critical differences: firstly, the new image showed that Arthur's shoulders, as we suspected, were far narrower, and there was no background space beyond the elbows, both confirming our hypothesis. Even more significant, however, was that the image ceased abruptly beneath Arthur's hands: unlike the other portrait there was no shelf on which he was resting. So what was this ledge doing in the picture at auction? It did not seem to be added, for there was no apparent line of joinery. But taking the Northumberland portrait as a lead, and mentally removing the breadth of the shelf, the two borders, and two inches from the top of the picture at auction, we now had the size of the lost royal image. This was thrilling progress. 'I bet you,' I said to Piers, 'that the shadow will not have found that!' As I said it, however, I realised it was a foolhardy challenge, and the subject was not pursued.

Although this latest arrival did not fully explain the discrepancies, we had gained a lot of ground. Furthermore, the emergence of an Elizabethan portrait 'type' of Arthur that in almost every crucial way showed the same painting, further shored up the identity of the picture at auction. It was the earliest visual corroboration, and within a hundred years of Arthur's lifetime. In other words, someone before Van der Doort had clearly also believed that this image represented Arthur, and lent validity to the claim.

By Tuesday, Piers had managed to establish a speculative link with the portrait's present owners and the Crown. In 1779 George, 6th Earl of Granard, married the daughter of Lady Elizabeth Hastings. With the marriage came chattel and estates from Elizabeth Hastings' father, the 9th Earl of Huntingdon, a family of ancient lineage and favoured friends of the crown. The 9th Earl had carried the Sword of State at the Coronation of George II, and his father, the 8th Earl, had borne the sceptre at George I's. The lost Royal Collection Arthur was last recorded in George I's reign and it is known that the King occasionally gave away objects from the Collection for which he felt he had no need. It was by no means a certain provenance, but as a hypothesis it fitted a treat. Why should not Arthur have found his way into the hands of key friends of the Crown? It was another possible piece to the jigsaw and by Wednesday morning, the day of the sale, we were in a position to act.

The auction room was densely packed. Piers and I sat four rows from the front, the lot was amongst the first twelve and we gained our seats ten minutes before the 10.30am commencement. I ran my eye suspiciously over the increasing swell of people – the familiar dealers, auction staff and collectors together with the abundance of new faces who appear at each sale. Some of them are vendors and their families coming to see their pictures sold, but there are others who just come to watch, or accompany friends, thereby increasing the audience and heightening the spectacle. I surveyed them all. Where might our unknown rival be? In my present state of mind nobody was above suspicion. I looked over to a group of dealers standing at the back, and one of them smiled – was that a smile of intent? I returned the greeting, and then kept my face squarely towards the rostrum in an attempt to blinker my growing paranoia. My mood was distinctly dangerous. I had fallen for this little picture, and the normal judgement I would use to consider an item for stock had been replaced by uncheckable acquisitive intent. I began to have visions of one of those crazy buyers that you occasionally see at auction, his buying paddle stalwartly erect, ignoring the competition with comic and perilous resolve.

This would not do. Inhaling deeply, I tried to focus rationally. There were still gambles. If this were to be the lost royal image, we still had to explain the size discrepancy. And if it were, how could we be sure that all the over-paint and additions would come off safely? Although I was buying this for myself, I did not want to over-pay for an object whose price I might one day need to recoup. Despite those sensible thoughts, by the time the lot number was announced, I had no idea what I was prepared to pay.

The bidding opened at £3,600. There were no offers immediately and, waiting a few seconds, I calmly raised my paddle. The auctioneer accepted my bid and then swiftly lifted his gaze above my head, and took another from the back of the room. Not wishing to be carried by a rapid upward momentum, I made him wait a few seconds before increasing it to £4,000. Taking care to continue this stalling pace, we continued steadily upwards – now at increments of £500 a time – my heart thumping almost audibly as we progressed. At £10,000 – around twice the upper estimate – it occurred to me that this buyer behind me was firmly on my tail, and I sensed a fierce challenge. No longer able to resist the urge, I turned round, and spotted him instantly. Paddle in hand, he was standing behind a group of dealers in the rear of the room. I also knew him. He was a collector of early-English panels – a leading figure in the music business who for the last few years had been assembling a discerning collection of Elizabethan and Tudor portraits. I had even sold him a number. Was he the shadow? I had no idea but this was bad news, as he was a man of considerable means. Turning back, I now prepared myself for open-ended expense.

At £11,500 the auctioneer looked to me for a bid of £12,000. At least, I thought, we were not yet going up by the normal increments of £1,000 a time at this level, and gave him a nod. Although it might make no difference to the final price, it offered mild solace that we were getting there more slowly. To my amazement the auctioneer then ceased to look behind me. He had encountered reluctance and was now responding by moving his eyes across the assembly for new bids. I braced myself for a fresh assault and looked over to the dealer with whom I had exchanged smiles, but he was busy talking to a colleague. 'I'm selling at £12,000,' the auctioneer then called, and began to tighten his knuckles around the head of the gavel in preparation. Where were the other buyers? What about the shadow? I could not believe I was now the only willing buyer, and half-shut my eyes, willing the sale to close. Somewhere in the background, I heard the hammer fall.

* * *

'You certainly pick 'em,' said Simon Gillespie, adjusting his standing lights so that their beam bore down mercilessly upon the diminutive image. When the chase has ceased, and before the next stage commences, there is often a glorious moment of respite, more often than not at my restorer's studio, when the object can be assessed safe in the knowledge that it is secured. Simon had been unable to see me till after work that evening, and the afternoon had been spent poring over the painting in a mood of both elation and apprehension. But it was only now, when I saw it under his lights, that I realised the quarry was now mine. A sense of tranquillity came with the realisation. For the time being, at least, it wasn't going anywhere, and the prize lay captive before me. That hiatus, however, does not last for long, and in this case it was even shorter. Now was the stage when its fate would be determined, and for this panel to be the lost royal picture, it would have to be transformed, and radically.

Working at his normal, steady and methodical pace, Simon unlatched the panel from the easel, placed it face down on his table, and tightened a pair of lenses round his head. He then reached up to the shelf above him for a scalpel, changed the blade, and rolled up his sleeves. 'Shall we begin?' I smiled, nodded, and he took the blade to the canvas on the back of the panel and began delicately to cut three sides of a small square, about two inches from the right-hand border. The operation took ten minutes, and he then gingerly turned back the flap with the side of the blade and, scraping away the remnants of glue, revealed a dark but distinct joint. It was the other side of the barely discernible line on the front of the panel – and joined two contrasting textures of wood. The differing grains now firmly testified that the wings had been added: it was different wood from a different date.

He then moved higher up and repeated the exercise – this time taking away a larger piece of canvas. 'It has also been added to on top,' he said. This was the news I was waiting for and I instantly craned forward to watch the flap being lifted back to reveal the lines of a flat-topped roof to the inner panel. At last, I thought, evidence we'd been waiting for – this had not been visible from the painted side, and I reached quickly for a ruler.

Taking a measurement from the top, I subtracted the height of the roof from the overall length. It was not enough, we had only lost an inch, so I asked Simon to try at the base. But despite removing most of the lower quarter of canvas, no additions were revealed. For this to be the royal picture we had to lose another three inches, and it now seemed unlikely that we would make any more revelations from the back of the panel.

I now urged Simon on to tackle the front. He complied by

dipping a swab-stick into a solution of diluted acetone, and applied it to a small area above Arthur's hat. He worked it with a gentle rolling action, rapidly removing the solvent with a hand-held swab of white spirit after each application. Many times he did this, gradually increasing the concentration of acetone as he did so. After the tenth or eleventh application the tip of the swab-stick turned brown. 'We're through to the first layer,' he announced, and from behind the blue-green film of grime shone a brighter, purer tone of blue, standing out from its discoloured surround. But despite the dramatic change, I had to remind myself that we were only cleaning off the first layer of grime and varnish, and that we had a formidable layer of over-paint to come.

Having established the minimum level of solvent required to remove the varnish layer, Simon then took a strip through Arthur's hat and on to his forehead, paying particular attention to the black pigment of his hat. Black is frequently a vulnerable pigment and can be removed accidently by cleaning, requiring extremely judicious cleaning methods. The cleaned strip promised great things to come. Although Simon had not yet tried to remove the over-paint on either the background or the lower face, I had not appreciated how dirty the picture was, and the startlingly bright line offered a radical change of tone. The black of the hat was crisper, and Arthur's forehead, which had not received the attentions of a later brush, possessed a glowing flesh tint. But I now exhorted Simon to dig into the later background to find out what lay beneath. Although it was past 9pm, I was banking on the fact that, like me, he was too carried away by excitement to worry about mundane things like food and sleep.

He rang his wife, gained an hour's extension, and returned to the operation. The present solvent would not be sufficient to cut through two-hundred-year-old paint, he explained, and he required something stronger. He surveyed a line of bottles on a shelf above his head and, muttering something incoherent, reached up, clinked his way to the back, and lifted down an antique glass vessel that did not look as though it had been opened for a decade. He then felt for another bottle and mixed a compound. I later discovered that this included a minute trace of ammonia.

In a very short time the tip of his solvent stick turned blue-green and a small area of the eighteenth-century blue over-paint above Arthur began to soften. He then stopped, and placed the panel beneath the lens of his microscope, angling the lights on to the tested centimetre. 'We're getting there,' he declared and made way for me to look. Through the lens at first all I could see were crusty particles of the dissolving top layer (we later discovered that it was ground lapis lazuli) but as I concentrated on the middle of the test I began to make out sparkling green dots of emerald intensity. We had struck Tudor England, and although barely visible with unmagnified sight, this hidden layer seemed solid and intact. Changing to a scalpel, over the next fifteen minutes Simon gradually scraped more of the later paint away to create a verdant gash, startlingly visible to the naked eye. I was now utterly transfixed, and quite unprepared for his sudden and abrupt halt: 'Hang on a moment. The green has stopped.' He sounded alarmed, and I anxiously examined his face for reassurance. But he remained bolted to his microscope, and he had now laid down his scalpel. I too became fearful. It was as if our patient's heart had stopped beating. Changing places, I looked down the lens into the green strip he had created (*Fig. 25*). The background had stopped. We had hit raw wood, getting on for an inch beneath the tip of the point of the inserted panel. Why there was plain wood around the inner panel, at this stage I did not know. But then it struck me that, on reflection, this development was perhaps not so serious. In fact, it could be what we were looking for. The implication was that the original painted image had here come to an end, and we were now going into the area around the actual picture itself.

We had also come to the end of Simon's tolerance. He was exhausted and expected home. 'Come back in three days,' he said. 'It'll be easier to do without you breathing down my neck, and I'll have a few more answers.'

I made another measurement with the ruler, and found we had reduced the image's size by a whole further inch. With another two to lose if our greatest hopes were to be realised, I went home to bed.

I think I had probably guessed the answer already, but when I next visited Simon he had an x-ray of the picture (*Fig. 26*) and had tested the paint on the shelf as well. The x-ray showed that Arthur in fact sat in a round-topped niche with wood above him. The wood showed signs of having been planed down, indicating that it had once been raised. The full story now presented itself. Arthur had once been in an integral frame: in other words the frame had been part of the panel; it was like a scooped out dish, and Arthur had been painted inside. In order to extend the panel, the frame had been planed down and painted over. The joiner had got round the problem of adding to the top of a curved-niche frame by clipping the curve to form two straight lines to which he could more easily adjoin a top section (*Fig. 27*). To increase the width of the panel, he had removed the right- and left-hand sides of the frame altogether, and attached new wings. And thus a late-medieval portrait of singular rarity had lain mutilated and disguised since the early eighteenth century.

And what about the extra two inches? Simon had done a cleaning test on the shelf to reveal that beneath it was planed wood – the base of the frame in fact. As the Northumberland copy had suggested, the shelf had never been part of the picture. The portrait of Arthur had stopped abruptly beneath his hands, and the frame had taken over.

'May I?' I asked Simon. He stood back to allow me to take the new measurement. We now had no more height to lose, but with this final revelation, perhaps no more was needed. As I lined up the ruler, I couldn't help thinking about Abraham Van der Doort, and the repetitions of history. He would have done the same, but if this were the missing picture, he would no doubt have lain the measure across the red and gold frame, peered into the niche, calculated the height, and recorded it with quill on to parchment. Three hundred and fifty years later, Simon, standing next to me with a ball-point pen and pad of restoration notes, was about to record the same measurement of a now frameless panel. I followed the indices of the ruler down to the exact point where the frame began, now clearly delineated by the revealed raw wood. I found that the base of the picture stopped abruptly on the division of an inch. Eleven inches. We had the dimensions of the lost royal image.

The borders had been attached with glue, later easily detached, and the picture was entirely stripped of all its later paint. An opulent green damask curtain hung behind Arthur, and when a filtering layer of over-paint had been removed, his robes shone brightly and evenly (*Fig. 28*). His expression became more gaunt, his pallor increased, and with it came a look of ominous frailty that forewarned of his untimely death. But within the vulnerability there was also beauty. Despite the conventions of Tudor art and kingly expectation, it seemed to express Arthur's humanity. Behind the rather weaselly gaze inherited from his father, and the wide-set eyes which he shared with his brother, was a look of heroic fragility.

We are unlikely ever to know the identity of the artist; he may well have been an itinerant Flemish resident in the English court and the name of a painter, almost certainly the same man, is variously recorded as 'Meynnart Wewiicke', 'Maynard, the King's painter' and 'Maynard Waynwyk'. The painting's importance, however, is not as a possible early Waynwyk, but as (so far) the only existing facial record of the heir to the Tudor throne, and which once belonged to the Crown itself.

I later commissioned a frame that attempted to combine Van

der Doort's description —'A reed *pintit* goulden' — with a similar frame on a picture in the Society of Antiquities. Visually, the lost heir to the Tudor throne has thus been restored. Why the Royal Collection portrait of Arthur, which appears, in fact, to be of his brother Henry at around the age of twenty, was renamed as Arthur as early as Henry's reign, can only be speculated. Henry stopped at nothing to find justifiable grounds for divorce from Catherine of Aragon so he could marry Anne Boleyn. He was utterly unscrupulous. The lusty-looking, so-called Arthur in the Royal Collection looked eminently up to the job of consummation: the one which I now owned did not. It is therefore just possible that the renamed portrait was used to help induce the incredulous into believing that Arthur had been mature enough to consummate his marriage, thereby rendering Henry's marriage to Catherine invalid, bearing in mind that the medieval Catholic church regarded marrying your brother's wife as incestuous. In this respect, the arrival of the true Arthur, in so honest and revealing a form, should perhaps not simply be seen as a fascinating addition to Tudor iconography. It may also add further nuance to an issue that radically affected the course of British history.

CHAPTER SIX

The Fresh Eye

THE MOST EFFECTIVE way to weigh up any work of art is without prejudice. If you ignore the label, the catalogue description, and the price estimate, forget the context and disregard the hype, often you will find the painting convincingly presents its own case. Allow yourself to be impressed by its immediate impact: a good piece of art, even if initially incoherent, should grasp the attention. Then, throw at it every vicious criticism you can think of. Make no excuses. Question the quality and description of form. Do the objects in a still life sit properly? Does the anatomy of a figure really work? Are the observations of nature in a 19th-century landscape *true,* or just facile effects? Ask yourself if there is anything new, worthwhile or revealing in what you see. Does what is on offer educate and enrich, or just pamper the senses?

It is an easy thing to write. The majority of prospective purchasers, however, will automatically suspend their assessment until they have read the catalogue and considered the estimated price and the story behind the work. But there is nothing better than first establishing an honest response, freed from the choking propaganda of the sales pitch and the context in which the painting finds itself. When applied by professionals, this approach has led to some remarkable discoveries.

One dealer who has turned this kind of independent thinking into a living is Gavin Graham. In 1989 he set the art world spinning with an unbelievable discovery from New York which left many dealers and experts bewildered: but it expressed more articulately than any theory what can be achieved with an open mind, and the importance of judging every object on its own terms. For Gavin Graham it was a further endorsement of an approach that has carried him profitably through the last twenty-five years.

Normally to be found standing at the back of the saleroom chatting to colleagues, Gavin attends almost every major art sale. He is of middling stature, with a boyish face, and until recently was never seen without his Loden cape which seemed to lend him a look of stealth. He moves around the international art world deftly and quietly, and has the uncanny ability of being simultaneously ubiquitous and inconspicuous — so successfully, in fact, that on one occasion he was locked in a Parisian antique shop overnight by the home-bound proprietor, who didn't realise that Gavin was still browsing. Now in his mid-forties, Gavin joined the art world when he was twenty, after graduating in history at Exeter University. Finding himself being sucked in the direction of his friends and contemporaries, most of whom were taking up stockbroking or estate agenting, he was instead far more impressed by his schoolfriend Chris Welby, a stall-holder in Portobello Road, who pulled off small but magnificent coups each Saturday from behind his barrow. He persuaded Welby to let him join him, and soon became absorbed in the market-trader's world. But he also realised after a time that he needed a more formal training, and so took the job on which many patriarchs of the art first cut their teeth: he became a saleroom porter, at Phillips in London. There, manhandling antique furniture and pictures behind the scenes in one of

London's main auction houses, his particular business strategy began to gestate. And it was on his honeymoon in France, a number of years later, that he had his first opportunity to see it work.

Gavin was strolling down a street in Nice in the South of France, arm in arm with his new wife, when he noticed an English portrait of a lady in one of the numerous overpriced antique shops. Having seen similar paintings sold on the London art market, he recognised it immediately as the work of Tilly Kettle, a collected 18th-century Anglo-Indian portraitist famous for his blocky faces which look as though they are recovering from the effects of dental surgery. The antique shop owner, however, had it described as by an anonymous artist, a decorative but unattributable English 18th-century portrait, and had consequently priced it cheaply. Gavin knew differently, and went straight to a telephone box to call up a dealer friend from London, who then came over on the next plane. Acting in partnership, they succeeded in purchasing the picture from the unwitting French proprietor, and its subsequent sale to the Tate Gallery, where, unlike France, Tilly Kettle is known and well regarded, amply paid for his honeymoon, and laid the foundations of his future commercial strategy. 'Strategy' may not be quite the right word for a skill that takes the form of canny commercial psychology. For Gavin has gone on to master a technique which many dealers use, but few apply to such devastating and comprehensive effect: to use City parlance, he is an arbitrageur in antique art.

Now based in a salubrious gallery in Notting Hill Gate, a stone's throw from the market street where he began as a stallholder twenty-five years earlier, Gavin has honed his approach to a level of almost scientific precision. His home is in Chiswick, and he is forever ready to leave by aeroplane from Heathrow airport twenty minutes away. He regards the Continent as a closer destination than Birmingham, a six-hour flight to New

York as no more arduous than a car journey to Edinburgh. Unlike most art dealers, he has not concentrated on creating a large network of private clients, but has instead formed a bank of international dealer friends on whom he continually draws – purchasing from the unappreciative, and selling to the receptive. Thus he will buy a 19th-century English picture of cats in a basket from an uncomprehending Italian old-master dealer, and sell it to a provincial art gallery specialising in Victorian art. He will travel to Holland for a sale of Dutch old masters, fish out a scene of the Beaufort Hunt, and then place it in an appropriate English sporting picture sale at Sotheby's. Forever alive to opportunities, and possessed of limitless energy, he draws on his cunning overview of the international market and a broad general knowledge of the differing commercial categories.

Gavin's greatest reward to date came in New York six years ago. America holds vast quantities of European art and antiques collected over the last century, and is today one of the main sources of supply for high-quality art and furniture dealers in Britain. Crate-loads of objects were brought over by émigrés from Europe and Britain over the last hundred years, as reminders of their homeland in the uncertain New World, and a great deal has also been sold to American collectors by dealers feeding a taste for fine art that was often rooted in the buyers' cultural origins. Many of the better pieces have fetched up in museums but, unlike in Britain, in America new museum directors and their trustees often decide to take new directions, selling or 'deaccessioning' objects in order to finance new acquisitions, and thereby supply the auctions with yet more booty. For the astute dealer, the American art market can be a rich source of stock.

Inspired by a catalogue of forthcoming pictures in a Sotheby's New York sporting sale, Graham decided he was ready for another American hunting trip. Taking the morning flight from Heathrow, he touched down in good time at JFK airport, and made the hour-long cab ride to central Manhattan, allowing himself an afternoon to view the main auctions. There was little to lift his spirits in the opulent salerooms of Sotheby's and Christie's: as is often the case, some items had looked far more enticing in the catalogue in London than in their physical reality in New York. Jet lag was now beginning to catch up, but resisting the urge to check in to his hotel, he instead hailed a cab and asked to go 59th Street on Lexington, to try his luck at Christie's secondary saleroom, Christie's East. Christie's East is the American equivalent of Christie's South Kensington where the cheaper lots, normally under $5,000 (£3,000), are offered at regular intervals throughout the year. Nothing like as chic an establishment as its grander older brother, where, like Sotheby's, many of the glamorous and well-heeled socialite wives of New York like to dwell and be seen, Christie's East caters more for the bulk of North American art and antique dealers. Walk through the bashed swing doors from the street and you are plunged into an atmosphere akin to backstage at a London theatre during rehearsal. More a frantic warehouse than a rarefied salon, faintly aggressive porters perpetually pack, log in and disgorge vast quantities of art and antiques through the industrial lifts and out to North America and the rest of the world.

The sale on view that day was American Art: that is, work by American artists, normally of American subjects, painted over the last 200 years. It seemed to Graham as he walked past the counters towards the pictures in the rear that this was probably the least likely place to find a sleeper. American art is not as mysterious as old masters. Most of the better artists are known and quite easily identifiable, if only through the signature and label. The collectors are in America, and so too are the appropriate experts and museums. The sales are attended by all the main specialist dealers in such things and visiting English art dealers feel about as potent as a horse trader at a car auction. But not wishing to go back home empty-handed, Graham decided he had nothing to lose by at least checking it out.

The pictures on view were hanging in a large cavernous room, brimming with American dealers. His eye passed over the scores of heads and across the hundreds of square feet of canvas that lined the walls – over two hundred pictures in all, mostly landscapes, in the warm orangey colouring that typifies their school. Initially there was nothing to excite him. Hanging in the far left-hand corner, however, one picture, whose shape, apart from anything else, was different from the other paintings (mostly landscapes), finally caught his interest. It was vertical, rather than horizontal, and in sharp contrast to the valley scenes and other genre subjects, was a stark, upright portrait of an 18th-century gentleman, with an attenuated neck and dislocated-looking jaw. Even an Englishman only needed half a second to identify it as the face known to every dealer in the room, indeed to almost the entire population of the United States, the visage that endorses every one-dollar bill, that of the father of modern America, George Washington (*Figs. 29 & 30*).

It would be fair to describe this historical portrait as the most famous in America. The series of original versions painted by the Anglo-American portrait painter Gilbert Stuart were the official portraits of the first President, and were copied and reproduced in their thousands, and later millions. Apart from the innumerable prints made of it, the image was also duplicated in oil by other painters during the 19th century, with varying degrees of success. Today, throughout the American auction market, these derivatives regularly come up for sale and if well enough painted, and sufficiently old, will be bought by collectors and dealers for anything from three hundred to a few thousand dollars.

This particular painting was viewed by Christie's as one of these later copies and dismissively described as 'American School' (i.e. painted by an unknown American at an unknown date) and given an estimate of $1,000–$1,500 (£700–£1,000). At this stage, however, Graham was not concerned with the estimate or description, which in any case he knew would be unremarkable, given the type of sale this was. He asked a porter to take the picture down for closer inspection. From two feet away it was the psychology of the portrait that hit him most powerfully: looking closely at the features, this was definitely an individual, he thought, an unapologetic rendering of a real face. The eyes were sunken and haunting, but retained a look of harsh dignity; the heavy shadows gave a skull-like appearance to the features but seemed to Graham to have the hallmark of an artist in complete control of his craft, one who was looking upon real bone and flesh. He thought back to other historical portraits he had seen in US museums and felt that, by contrast, this had the tough authenticity of the eyewitness account, an authentic portrait, unlike the plethora of mute copies that fill the auction houses of America. He placed it on the floor and took another long look, this time from across the room. The face lost none of its power: if anything, it gained some.

This, he reflected, had considerable possibilities. A similar picture by Gilbert Stuart had made a lot of money a few years earlier at Bonhams in London, and he calculated that by buying this one cheaply, and placing it in an English sale – as opposed to an American specialist auction in New York – even if it were not an original Stuart, this would excite English dealers. If *he* felt so positive, why shouldn't others also? Again, Gavin was relying on his innate understanding of the market's psychology. In America, knowledgeable buyers would automatically, and per-haps rightly, view this as yet another later copy of their most famous icon. But a portrait of Washington, of this quality, loosely catalogued in the right country sale in England, could cause a wave of curiosity from London and local dealers who would then be prepared to risk a substantial bid.

There was also another possible bonus he hardly dared think about. What if this *were* an original by Stuart, and it had been passed by? It was a wild card he couldn't count on, but nor could he rule it out either. He looked again at the face. All the paint appeared original, and the picture had been recently cleaned and relined, so at least there would be no hidden damages to be revealed by removing dirt and over-paint; equally, there were no hidden qualities to be revealed by cleaning either. What he saw was what was on offer – there was no apparent mystery to this 'American School' Washington. And yet, as everyone must be able to see, the painting was so good. He recalled later that the feeling worried him. Why shouldn't it be real? On the other hand, how on earth could it be?

Ask any successful dealer why he or she comes up with a final figure they would be prepared to pay for an object, and while they might offer you a breakdown of costs associated with cleaning, restoration, framing and business overheads, it is often a feeling from the pancreas that finally decides the matter. It makes attending auctions a frighteningly risky business because sometimes the pancreas dominates, rational assessment is forfeited and the hand stays up. Enormous prices are then paid for objects which are too expensive to move on for a profit. Although Gavin Graham had a high regard for the portrait, he did not at this stage feel it was a definite sleeper. All he was certain of was that its quality was significantly better than the catalogue implied, and that there was definite potential for a lucrative transaction of the type in which he specialised. He would sleep on it, he thought, and ring up the following day with a firm bid.

What he didn't know then was that Christie's had checked out the picture before they put it in the sale. The vendor, whose identity Christie's has never revealed, had consigned it some months before the sale and allowed the auction house enough time to send a photograph to a Gilbert Stuart expert, Marvin Sadik. Auction houses often defer to specific experts and Sadik was the obvious man to go to. As an ex-director of the National Portrait Gallery of America, the iconography of Washington fell squarely into his area of academic interest. Sadik wrote back to Christie's indicating that he needed to see the picture itself, and was not sufficiently convinced of its status to commit himself on the evidence of a photograph. The circumstances of its attribution are obscure, but by the time of the sale Christie's were certain of one thing: this portrait of Washington was not by the American master himself, but nothing more than an anonymous copy.

Gavin was so busy visiting other dealers over the next two days that he clean forgot to ring up and leave a bid. It was not till lunchtime of the day of the sale that it suddenly came back to him. He was in the middle of his second course, talking to a friend about the state of the art market, when the recollection hit him mid-mouthful. The figure of $8,800 came to him – at least that would knock out the uncommitted, casual interest – and with half an hour to go before the lot was offered, he telephoned to leave the bid with the Christie's clerk, and returned to lunch. Three quarters of an hour later, after he had finished his coffee, he then rang them again for the result. It had been acquired by his commission bid, for $3,000 (£2,000), and Gavin triumphantly returned to the table to say goodbye to his friend. For those who have had experience trading with Gavin, this was a typical business lunch.

He was bemused by the price. Clearly nobody had thought it was genuine, otherwise he wouldn't have bought it for less than his $8,800 bid. And yet it was twice as much as Christie's had estimated. Someone else, he surmised, had reckoned it a little bit better than the pejorative 'American School' attribution given it in the catalogue.

Still uncertain as to what he had bought, Gavin had the picture shipped to England, and two weeks later was able to uncrate it on the floor of his Notting Hill Gate gallery. At this point, before he had seen it again, he recalls that he was very happy to have bought it, but 'was not jumping up and down'. All too often exciting paintings bought in the heated, competitive environment of a New York sale can look distinctly underwhelming when unwrapped in the cold light of a London shop. Not so, however, with his Washington as he tore away the final layer of brown paper. The same powerful presence that had seduced him in the crowded New York saleroom worked its magic on him again in London. He propped it up against the wall and continued to marvel. Wherever he placed it, in the dark, in daylight or under the gallery lights, the painting's unerring presence resonated.

As he was moving the picture over to the window he noticed the labels on the back for the second time. He then realised that he had not yet considered their possible significance – a strange oversight for a dealer, for they can often contain more information about authenticity and provenance than can be read from the front. At the top of the stretcher, in a 19th-century hand on a yellowing label, was the name of 'Coles'. It meant nothing to Gavin but he realised that should it be required, there was an outside chance that this could reveal a provenance, the name of a collection, perhaps, in which the painting had once hung.

The next day he had the picture delivered to Sotheby's in London, marked for the attention of James Miller, Head of British Pictures. Uncertain how to proceed with the research, Gavin knew that the picture department in Bond Street with its library and researchers would have a greater chance of finding out more. He began to feel that what he had first viewed as an interesting and potentially profitable speculation, destined for a country auction house where other dealers might chance their bids, deserved more thorough investigation. Could it possibly be by the hand of Stuart himself? Sotheby's would no doubt have a view, and he now awaited their reaction.

Three days later he had a call from Miller. He told him to go immediately to a library and get hold of a book entitled *The Life Portraits of Washington and their Replicas* by Morgan and Fielding. 'You might also,' he added, 'learn a little more about that name Coles. Look particularly at number fifty-three.' His tone was excited. Gavin closed the shop at once and made straight for the Witt Library. It took him ten minutes to reach the Adam-designed building in Portland Square, and another half hour to locate the slim volume published in 1931. Dry-mouthed with anticipation thanks to Miller's oblique remark, he turned to page 174 and there, under Catalogue No. 53, was the description of a now lost Stuart portrait that had been commissioned and owned by James Madison, 4th President of the United States in the first quarter of the 19th century. He followed the provenance downwards. The portrait had hung at his home, Montpelier House, in Virginia and then passed to his wife, Dorothy Dodd Payne. After she died, he read, it was bequeathed to Madison's private secretary who went on to become Governor of Illinois. Madison's secretary was a judge, by the name of Edward Coles. By the time of the book's writing, the painting had travelled by descent to the possession of his granddaughter, Miss Mary R. Coles of Philadelphia and was still with the family. The yellow label on the back of the picture had thereby unlocked the painting's history.

Ironically, it was Marvin Sadik, the very man who saw a photograph of the portrait first time round from Christie's, who now confirmed to Sotheby's that this was indeed the lost Madison portrait of George Washington by Gilbert Stuart, lost for fifty years. A major re-addition to the Washington iconography, it was a particularly animated example of Stuart's work, derived from a sitting he had with the President in his studio at Germanstown, Pennsylvania in 1796. Another aspect in its favour was its tremendous condition; although re-lined with new canvas to support the aged old one, the paint surface was in near-pristine order and showed little or no signs of abrasion or over-cleaning.

Gavin gave the painting to James Miller for sale at Sotheby's and I remember meeting him on the day of the auction. Word had got out that he had pulled off an historic coup in a New York sale, from under the noses of the whole American trade, and that the prize was now hanging in Sotheby's for all to see. The department had placed an enticingly low estimate of

£30,000–£50,000, which all knew to be unrealistically low for so significant an icon of American history. As is his habit, Gavin was lurking at the back of the saleroom, and in his Loden cape and small moustache, looking pale, reflective and triumphant all at once, had the appearance of a war-shy musketeer. He told me that he had been to the solicitor that day to finalise his divorce proceedings, and his normal bravado had been somewhat dampened by the experience. 'He gives with one hand – and takes with the other,' he whispered to me as he left the auction, after his lot had sold.

Washington was bought over the telephone by a commercial American art gallery, who may indeed have viewed the picture when it came up – mis-catalogued – first time round in New York. If they did, then this time they were more bullish. They paid £250,000.

* * *

It is an interesting truth that some of the most obvious discoveries can only be made by those who are not at all close to them. They need the benefit of objectivity. It took an Englishman to spot the intrinsic quality in a painting of one of America's most familiar icons, and little more than a year later, another Englishman, the Duke Street old-master dealer Derek Johns, caused a similar wave of native embarrassment, this time in Vienna.

As a specialist in old masters, Derek had showed promise from the start. In 1964, at the age of twenty-six, he became the youngest ever Director of Sotheby's, and shortly afterwards was elevated to head of department. In 1981 he left the firm to start his own gallery, rapidly establishing himself as one of the leading players in the old-master trade. The time he devotes to tracking down major old masters is encroached upon only by his love of cooking, and in 1993 he set the art world agog by winning the BBC *Masterchef* award with a *tour de force* main course of rosettes of turbot in leek sauce.

On the morning of 13th November 1990, he was flipping through a stack of sale catalogues on his desk, an accumulation that had built up over the previous weeks while he had been travelling on business in America and on the Continent, and towards the bottom of the pile he came across one from the Dorotheum – Vienna's leading and state-owned auction house for fine art. The catalogue had been waiting on his desk for the last week, and the sale was the very next day. With the agility of a chef at morning market, and aware of the need to react quickly should there be anything of interest, his eye rapidly picked its way across all that was on offer, searching for items of potential that he could then instruct his agent in Vienna, Roman Herzig, to look at in the flesh that very afternoon.

Lot 262, illustrated in colour, stopped him dead (*Fig. 32*). The painting was attributed to Guido Cagnacci, an artist who worked in Vienna in the middle years of the 17th century, and its size alone implied a work of monumental importance: it was 4 × 3 metres. The scene depicted was one from Pagan history and depicted Diana (seated back right) discovering the pregnancy by Jupiter of her nymph Callisto (recumbent lower left). Although the canvas was scored and creased, suggesting – as is the fate of many large, unhouseable works – that it had been rolled up for storage, Derek was instantly struck by the painting's evident quality. Even from the illustration he could not help but be impressed by the subtle lighting and colouring, the graceful anatomy and the complex positioning of the figures. He could not immediately place it, but he had seen this style before, and it was certainly not Cagnacci – that concerned him rather. Furthermore, the estimate of 120,000 Austrian schillings (about £1,000) seemed at odds with the fact that the picture was illustrated almost full-page, and in colour – a treatment usually reserved for far more expensive works. He guessed that the auction house was also somewhat fazed, and realising it was a significant work, but being unable to come up with more than a perhaps tentative attribution to Cagnacci, and for want of something firm had left it to the market to make up its own mind on true authorship and price. In this respect it had worked, for Derek was now thinking hard.

Just as he was about to lift a telephone to Roman Herzig in Vienna, to ask for his on-the-spot reaction, it came to him. On occasions such as this, an attribution will sometimes flash up, unbidden and at electric speed. It should perhaps be seen as the rightful reward of a prepared mind, but no computer, library, or delegated researcher can match the potency of informed, instinctive response, born out of the hard experience of constantly sifting through the market's offerings and the lessons of financial risk. An international art dealer will see hundreds of thousands of pictures every year in museums, galleries and amongst the stock of other traders. Some he will deliberately commit to memory, others he might absorb unconsciously. At times of need, with deadlines fast approaching, this quality of intuitive recollection is often the distinguishing trait of the successful art dealer or auctioneer.

A friend of Derek's, an American academic by the name of Dwight C. Miller, had been working of late on a book about the eminent Bolognese painter, Marcantonio Franceschini (1648–1729) and Derek had taken an interest in the project. The artist had particularly captured Derek's imagination because not only was he a leading painter of the period, but also the most successful art dealer, selling major works by the Italian masters Guercino and Reni. Miller's book was taking as its central focus what the author saw as one of the 'most engrossing episodes in the history of Baroque Italian painting and art patronage' – Franceschini's decoration of the state rooms in the Garden Palace of the House of Liechtenstein in Vienna. The works were commissioned by Prince Johann Adam Andreas at the turn of the 18th century, and consisted of two spectacular cycles of gigantic wall paintings – one featuring Adonis and the other

Diana – constituting a high point in Vienna's art history. As fashions altered, late-19th-century Viennese taste could no longer stomach all this archaic baroque excess, and the paintings were deaccessioned at the beginning of this century. All, with the exception of one, had ended up in the Prince of Liechtenstein's collection in his modern principality in Vaduz, four hundred miles away. Remembering images of the artist's work, and the fact that an important painting was lost, Derek felt convinced that the illustration he was looking at was none other than this missing picture.

He now telephoned Roman Herzig in Vienna with more specific intent. Roman had viewed the sale, he told Derek, but had not noticed the picture because it was rolled up. Now he hotfooted it back to have a look. A few hours later he reported back to Derek that although the picture had suffered physically, it was of outstanding quality and most certainly in recoverable condition. The following day, encountering little or no competition, Derek bought it for the equivalent of £1,000.

Dwight Miller authenticated the picture and excitedly welcomed its return, and four months later Roman sold it to the Prince's collection for $300,000 (£200,000) where it will join its fellow members of the Diana cycle. When Derek last asked, it was still being restored.

Just as in the case of the George Washington portrait in America, here is another extraordinary example of a country's own experts being unable to recognise a vital piece of national heritage on their own doorstep. Their senses somehow become numbed to the familiar and it takes a fresh, albeit expert view from a different culture and sensibility to realise what in retrospect appears obvious. It also happens within our own art establishment.

Thomas Williams, a thirty-five-year-old London art dealer in old-master drawings, decided to train as an artist when he left Eton, and only in his late twenties gave up producing his own works in favour of selling those by others. But the technique of looking, assessing and comprehending – the essential skills of an artist – have stayed with him as a trader, giving him the superior insights of a poacher turned gamekeeper. Knowing how it is done allows him to understand the best, and reject the worst, with the benefit of a practitioner's insight.

Tom is forever on the move, either exhibiting at international art fairs or visiting museums and clients, and in the middle of 1994 found himself at Edinburgh's National Gallery. The austere sandstone edifice is an integral part of Scotland's heritage, holding examples of some of the greatest old-master paintings in the world, as well as some of the best of its early national art. Tom was there to discuss possible acquisitions from his stock with one of the curators, and had left sufficient time beforehand to browse through the photographic library of their exhibits – an economic way of surveying the collection without trudging down corridors and heaving around the portfolio boxes in which the drawings are kept.

Tom's particular interest is Italian old-master drawing, and it was to photographs of these that he was particularly drawn. He knew that there was a interesting work by the 16th-century Genoese artist Lazzaro Tavaroni in the collection and so he looked in the drawer for the letter 'T'. The artist he came to as he browsed through the drawer of photographs immediately before Tavaroni was Agostino Tassi, a recognised but not overly distinguished 17th-century landscape draughtsman. He pulled out a photograph accidentally, not knowing at first what he was meant to be looking at. It was a scant but spirited study in ink of saplings on a hillock, with a small figure half way up on the left.

He identified the drawing immediately, rather as one instantly knows the sender of an unopened letter by the writing on the envelope. He had come across this particular 'vocabulary of marks', as he calls it, before but certainly not in connection with Tassi. Artists will develop their own idioms for describing the

physical reality before them, a coherent visual language which is entirely their own, and from which attributions can later be made. As an artist and dealer himself, Tom is perhaps more aware of this than most, empathising with the process of translation from three dimensions into two – in other words the act of drawing and painting – and his recognition was instant. The airy, dashed-off lines, curls, commas and strokes, often no more than perfunctory outlines, were the idiosyncratic but effective techniques employed by one of the earliest landscape draughts-men in Italy, the contemporary of Leonardo da Vinci, Fra Bartolomeo. He then turned the photograph over and saw that it was described as the 'circle of Agostino Tassi'.

Although executed in a highly distinctive style, the curatorial staff had been slow to spot an extremely important artist's work in their collection because they had not approached it, as Tom had done, with a fresh and serendipitous eye. It could happen in any museum or art gallery. 'Now you say it, of course it seems so obvious,' said one of them later. Tom immediately told the curator he had come to visit and a photograph was dispatched to Chris Fischer, Keeper of Prints and Drawings at the Royal Museum of Fine Arts in Denmark, and the authority on Fra Bartolomeo's works. In a written reply he expressed his pleasure at the emergence of a new work by the artist, datable to the '1490s or early 1500s'.

This sort of oversight is surprisingly easily made. I first noticed the phenomenon at university. While doing a thesis on an obscure arts-and-crafts pottery, active at the turn of the century, I visited the home of an expert who had spent a number of years exhaustively collating every available example of the pottery's work. Hanging on the wall of his house was a tile, unques-tionably by the pottery, which he had bought many years before in a local junk shop. Despite his highly focused work on all the available material in museums and private collections, he had become blind to the familiar, and was completely unaware that he too owned a piece! He was quite shaken by the revelation. As with the other examples in this chapter, the anecdote reinforces the truism that the obvious is often overlooked. And this will undoubtedly remain a basic, unchanging characteristic of human nature. So too, therefore, will these often bewildering discoveries continue to be made.

CHAPTER SEVEN

Behind the Gavel

FOR TWO WEEKS in early December 1988, a High Court judgement was causing sleepless nights for many fine-art auctioneers.
A Surrey auction house, Messenger May Baverstock, had sold a
pair of paintings three years earlier in one of their regular sales.
Within six months they turned up at another auction house,
completely re-catalogued, and made a hundred times more.
Much to the art world's disbelief, Messenger's were now ordered
to make up the full difference to the first owner.

Although this was later disputed, the paintings, of two fox-
hounds on a rocky seashore, had been re-established as the work
of the celebrated horse painter, George Stubbs. When sold first
time round, they had been catalogued by Messenger's as 'English
School', with no attribution to a painter, and an estimate of
£30–£50. They had made £840, more, indeed, than was expected
– but considerably less than they made five months later when
they came up at Sotheby's London, fully described as works
by the master, and subsequently purchased for £88,000. The
distressed former owner, Penelope Luxmoore-May, was awarded
£76,222, which was the difference between the two prices,

including interest, and minus insurance and commission. Although Messenger's had taken steps to research the pictures, the judge declared that the auctioneers had failed to exercise 'reasonable skill and care' in their valuation and sale, and were therefore entirely liable for the consequent notional loss to Mrs Luxmoore-May.

This was chilling news for provincial fine-art auctioneers, and appeared to open the floodgates not only for future claims but also for *retrospective* claims for mis-cataloguing. Although undisclosed compensation was already sometimes offered in such cases, as with the Chester del Piombo, the obligation now seemed stringently enshrined in law, with extreme financial consequences. What was particularly galling, however, was that the Court seemed unaware of the difficulties and complexities of attribution that face a commercial cataloguer. Messenger's instantly appealed.

Two weeks later, on 21st December, the Court of Appeal overturned the judgement. Conceding that the Luxmoore-Mays deserved sympathy, as did anyone who had 'unwittingly parted with a sleeper', it was felt that the judgement had rested too heavily on the issue of whether the paintings were by Stubbs (and both at the time of the trial, and afterwards, this attribution was doubted) and not enough on the evidence of negligence; in attempting to establish the hounds' value and authorship, Messenger's had also sought the advice of a fine-art consultant, and claimed to have taken them to London for an over-the-counter appraisal from a London auction house. Neither, it was stated, had rated their value or recognised the artist, and on reflection Messenger's were therefore deemed to have taken sufficient professional pains not to be negligent in law. This was an enormous relief, not only for Messenger's, but for many others in the auction trade, who had felt that insufficient account had been taken of the problems facing the fine-art cataloguer.

The appeal also had the useful effect of clarifying the exact nature of a country fine-art auctioneer's obligations. The judges acknowledged that country salerooms abound with similar sorts of works, and that they are very often derived or copied from the works of major artists. When Messenger's sold them, the pictures were very dirty and by the time they came up at Sotheby's had been substantially cleaned. Bearing this in mind, the court went on to establish that the obligation for country auctioneers is similar to that for general practitioners. For a specialist it may be different, both in medicine and art, but it was decided that attribution was like diagnosis, not an exact science, and providing that every reasonable skill and effort had been employed in getting it right in the 'presented circumstances', the auctioneer was off the hook. This allowed for differing views on attribution, or even wrong ones. It did, however, imply that there was no excuse if proper research was not undertaken. It could also be inferred that a major London auctioneer, with more specialist expertise at his fingertips, had even less excuse for error.

So far in this book we have dealt largely with those who use salerooms to supply them with opportunities – the hunters who lie in wait, and then combine judgement with risk to secure the sleeper from an unknowing auction house and competitors. This leaves out the other side, the auctioneers themselves, a different species of trader, but equally active in the game of discovery. The auctioneer, as agent, is often seen as on a par with an estate agent or stockbroker – the higher the price he achieves for the client, the better it is for both, and this offers reassurance to a hesitant vendor. When they first come on the market, the majority of pictures pass through the auctioneers' hands – often vendors are drawn to the main salerooms by glossy marketing and publicity material. But with this advantage, the auctioneers also face incumbent responsibilities and concerns, and the issue of the sleeper ranks high amongst them.

A sleeper *per se* is not as much of a worry as one that passes unnoticed by all but the hawk-eyed buyer, who then sells it on for a large profit. For if more than one person spots it, the sleeper may well be bid up to its proper price. Sometimes, indeed, when two or more buyers spot a sleeper, the adrenaline of discovery, and the commercial advantages to a dealer of buying a picture whose real identity is not documented in the open marketplace (making it 'fresher goods' when it comes to selling on), mean that it will sometimes make even more than if it were fully and properly catalogued! This, however, is not an ideal state of affairs. When an owner consigns a picture to auction, he has entrusted it to the experts' scholarship and commercial skills, and this burdens the auctioneer with an obligation to establish if not the right artist then at least the work's approximate value. With the volume of pictures that pass through the auctioneers' hands, however, it is not an easy task to be always right, and for as long as there is auction business, sleepers will continue to happen. This is not a reflection on the quality of cataloguing: it is a symptom of the market's prodigious size. With the tens of thousands of pictures that are milled through the auction system each year, it is only to be expected that some will pass by unrecognised. It would be commercially naïve to expect otherwise.

Nevertheless, the sleeper is still a phenomenon which the auctioneer strives to avoid. The legal implications have been discussed, but it is also a matter of public perception. On a personal level, the cataloguer does not like to be seen as missing an obvious attribution for the entirely straightforward reason that it hurts professional pride. On a corporate level, the auction house is not that keen on it either: the main auction rooms compete fiercely to be shown in a good light. They would much prefer this natural occurrence to happen at the auction room down the road, rather than in their own front garden.

The mainstream art auction rooms therefore require high-quality experts, and one such expert is Charles Beddington. In the early '80s he was taken on by Christie's, an auction house which had realised how much auctioneering had changed, and that the issue of proper cataloguing was becoming critical. Recruited to respond to the problem, Charles was then described variously as a 'troubleshooter' and, contradictorily, as 'the last line of defence', but he prefers instead to settle for the cricketing metaphor of 'long-stop'. His job initially was to prevent public embarrassments by improving the quality of cataloguing, or, to use his own imagery, to be there at the edge of the field when the ball has winged past the wicket-keeper and is heading ignominiously towards the boundary. Although his job later increased to incorporate much more, his function then was to make sure that a work of art never became a sleeper; if it did, he considered himself to have failed.

When Charles joined Christie's at the age of 23 in 1983, the art world was metamorphosing dramatically, and nowhere was the change more evident than in the auction rooms. Although the process had begun a number of decades earlier, art and antiques were becoming unequivocally acknowledged as big business on a par with real estate, and Sotheby's and Christie's, quoted businesses, were now lined up against each other in furiously competitive combat to secure major collections and works of art. Their commercial personae had changed: no longer were they the backroom suppliers to dealers, as they had been before the war, but extroverts, voraciously reaching out to the end user – the private buyer. Consequently their catalogues became more 'user friendly' – lavishly produced, with colour illustrations on every page of a major sale catalogue, replacing black-and-white illustrated catalogues, which in turn had taken the place of the frugal written descriptions, rarely with illustrations, of a decade or so earlier. But this brought with it problems. If a work was mis-catalogued, it would no longer slip through unnoticed, but in an explosion of publicity. The term 'sleeper', which had been used since the '60s to describe dormant communist spies within the Establishment, was borrowed to denote pictures which had passed by unrecognised in the art establishment, and with the auction houses' new high profile, this was deliciously newsworthy.

Avoiding sleepers required a radical upgrade in the quality of cataloguing. Up to this point experts were inclined to be generalists, and in a single day's work were expected to come up with intelligent suggestions about anything – from a Victorian crofting scene to a 16th-century martyrdom, a Dutch still life to a sporting scene by Stubbs. Their knowledge was therefore often formidably broad, but inevitably could not embrace detailed knowledge of every subject. In the increasingly specialised modern art market, this could have massive commercial consequences. A studio-of-Van Dyck portrait of the young Charles II, for example, may be worth £10,000, but a fully authentic work – and the difference is only fathomable with a profound understanding of the paint technique – could fetch £1,000,000: to a non-specialist eye, particularly when dirty, they could look exactly the same. These old-style experts were also expected to be business-getters as well, and a conscious attempt was made to find the aristocratic and socially adept, who could effortlessly reassure their relations and neighbours of the merits of going to auction. Given the enormous amount of art in the hands of the gentry and aristocracy, and their inherent tendency to deal with their own kind, a further expectation of the expert, and a consideration in his recruitment, was that he therefore be of the right pedigree as well.

In the changed market, however, experts had to be more scholarly to cope with the new demands. Staff with a title, a country pile, and a network of grand relations were still both useful and necessary, but the auction houses required top-class intellectual back-up as well. Scholarship across the board was now not only freely available, but more vital in a sophisticated market that expected the auctioneers to be able to advise on, and dispose of, their treasured objects with the utmost academic skill. The auction houses still wanted people who could feel at ease with the clients they were catering for, but above all they now needed brains. The cleverest available were therefore actively sought out, recruited and fostered. Graduate trainee schemes, introduced by Christie's in 1986, took the best Art-History graduates available, many from Cambridge, and attempted to turn them into first-class auctioneers in an aggressive and expanding market. To be gentrified greatly helped but the men, and occasionally women, they recruited were more crucially expected to contribute intelligence to the new campaign.

In many ways Charles fitted the profile of the new-style auction expert Christie's began to recruit in 1983 perfectly. His family background was artistic, rather than grand. He came from a tradition of music lovers, and over lunch with me he whimsically recalled that his great-grandmother was seen off on her honeymoon by Puccini and Caruso. Charles nurtured an interest in culture and art from an early age. His uncle, who bequeathed him his art library, worked for the leading art dealers Wildenstein, and his aunt, who also has a passion for pictures and still makes regular visits to Christie's to check up on him, first took Charles to the National Gallery at the age of eight. On a trip to New York at the age of eleven, he spent all his pocket money on every available postcard in the Metropolitan Museum. Ironically, however, when it came to leaving school, he did everything to avoid pursuing art as a vocation. He began by studying English Literature at London University and was taught Milton by A. S. Byatt – but even this auspicious tutelage was not enough to divert him from the destiny that had begun to take shape in the postcard shop of the Metropolitan, and after a year he found himself switching to the Courtauld Institute to study Art. He still, however, considered alternatives, and spent a few months making what he now earnestly describes as 'seriously good' sandwiches for a Covent Garden snack bar. But it was a vain attempt to ignore a temperament and conditioning that were leading him ineluctably towards the art world, and a few months later he was interviewed by Christie's. For the role they had in mind, he fitted the bill, and was immediately accepted.

Somewhat in awe of his new surroundings, Charles gained a taste of what was expected of him in the first week. He recollects finding himself seated between two aristocrats. 'They showed me a landscape by some obscure 17th-century Dutch painter and asked me for my view. It was a little out of my area, and I hesitated, saying that I might well have seen something similar in the Wallace collection, but I was not sure. I should keep that quiet if I were you, said one of them. We've been led to believe you know all about these things.'

Knowing about things, or more particularly European old masters, is what Charles's job is all about. He can now be defined as one of the academic centres of the organisation, dividing his job between amassing works for their regular old-master sales and simultaneously following an intense personal commitment to making sure that pictures are thoroughly and accurately catalogued. He is regarded as something of an eccentric, a fanatic and also an old-fashioned sexist who sets his own agenda and prefers to work at night rather than by day, when he can be alone with his books and freed from what he describes as the 'cacophony of phone calls and distracting presence of a secretary's legs'. When old-master paintings needing research are located or brought to the front counter, Charles is often required, particularly in the case of uncertain attributions, to bring his skill, books and rolodex of specific authorities to bear, in the shortest possible time, upon the subject in question.

* * *

With people like Charles safe behind their book-covered desks, the other side of the business, the procuring of works of art, is left to those with different skills. One method, pioneered in the early '70s with immediate success, is the now famous 'roadshow' technique. Known more technically in the business as a 'probe', this is when a group of clean-cut general experts, covering the range of art and antiques, intrepidly set themselves up in a hotel in the regions or abroad and, with the benefit of advance publicity, wait for the locals to bring in heirlooms for appraisal which they might later be able to sell. The experts are sometimes divided up into generic areas of responsibility: there will be someone covering what has been dubbed 'knobbly art', which is anything such as furniture or sculpture that is upright and three-dimensional but does not necessarily include china, silver and jewellery which sometimes have their own specialists. There is also an expert for 'flat art' which embraces all categories of picture – oil painting, watercolour, drawing, prints and photographs and he or she may have to assess anything from an old-master landscape to a collection of dirty postcards. According to the venue's regional speciality, or strength, the team might also include someone for oriental art or possibly 'collectables' such as toys. If an object emerges which is commercial enough, and the expert's technique is sufficiently reassuring, they might then secure it for sale.

Referred to rather caustically as 'the art world's answer to pet's corner' by less charitable members of the organisation, the roadshow process can be utterly exhausting for the experts themselves, who over the course of the day are expected to make instant and informed judgements on scores of artworks placed before them, and occasionally to disabuse owners of their heady optimism – a process that has even been known to end in violence when the poor owner is told by a smart-talking Londoner in a suit, that their cherished artefact is a worthless piece of junk (or 'NSV' – no sale value – as the euphemism goes!).

So much time is wasted looking at unsuitable objects that the main auction houses will now often get their regional representatives to locate the main collections or likely vendors first, and the London expert, with specific appointments, will then follow. The probes are still necessary in some of the less well-covered regions, however, and as one old hand at the process (who wishes to remain anonymous) has put it, 'Being polite for seven hours a day can feel close to Hell.' A trick occasionally employed to explain to an ambitious owner that their object is not suitable for sale is to damn it with praise: 'Madam, it is such a beautiful piece, surely it would be a shame to part with it?' Other experts, reaching the point of exasperation when unable to satisfy an insistent owner, have been known to resort to extreme measures. One bemused owner of a fake 17th-century flower picture was unable to find the name of the artist to whom the expert had attributed it in any books in the local library. The librarian had to tell her that the name of the 'artist' she had been given, Hertz Van Rental, was in fact a service offered by the international car-hire company.

It is a job which requires psychology, stamina, courage and tact if it is to be done well, particularly as the experts don't always have all the answers. At the same time they are required to keep a sharp eye out for commercial opportunities – the very purpose of the exercise after all – and it can be a long and punishing day.

White settler cultures in Africa had sometimes proved to be a rich, and comparatively less thoroughly tapped source of art and antiques than Europe. In an uncertain political climate, the art world had also witnessed a tendency amongst the white population to turn chattels into hard currency when the opportunity was presented, and it was decided by the higher powers at Christie's that South Africa, with its wealthy ex-British and ex-Dutch populations, was a land of opportunity which had not been sufficiently alerted to the advantages of 'expert fine-art appraisal' – and Christie's in particular. So, in March 1985, four of their experts were duly dispatched to the Sandton Sun Hotel in Johannesburg, an appropriately dignified location in the capital, and then on to the Mount Nelson Hotel in Cape Town in order to 'probe' the country.

* * *

Looking after the 'flat art' was Henry Wyndham, a more than accomplished probing ambassador for the company in South Africa. A giant old Etonian with impeccable social connections and an impressive patrician bearing, somewhat softened by a sheepdog-ish haircut, Henry was a combination of both the 'old' and 'new' Christie's man. Although his first job was two weeks as an assistant gardener to the Queen Mother at Clarence House, he had later taken to commerce, and the art world, with precocious vigour. At the age of twenty-five he was appointed a Vice President of Christie's New York, where he pioneered the concept of British sporting sales, and returned to England shortly afterwards to a main-board directorship, with particular responsibility for Victorian pictures. A combination of connoisseurship, urbanity and flair has turned him into one of the young patriarchs of the auction world.

The team was coming to the end of its mission, and the afternoon was melting into evening. The trip had proved unproductive so far: Johannesburg had not yielded the treasures they had hoped for and Cape Town was also beginning to look depressing. All Henry had been able to muster by the end of the first day of the second leg was a collection of Polaroid snaps of lacklustre landscapes by minor or unidentifiable hands, purchased by South Africans from British dealers before the war. The queue had died down, and just as they were about to retire to the hotel bar, two photographs were dropped on Henry's table by a man with a strong Dutch accent. Glancing at them with a slightly jaundiced eye – it had been a long day, and he was looking forward to its end – Henry's mood immediately lightened. He had been presented with a pair of Venetian views, canal scenes bordered by large Venetian palazzi. 'On looking at them more carefully,' he recalled, 'I was gobsmacked. And then I thought, this is too good to be true.' For the one artist these photographs instantly transmitted to Henry was Antonio Canaletto, the supremely able painter of Venice in the 18th century, and whose works were insatiably bought by the British on their Grand Tours of Italy. Many of his paintings now line the walls of British stately homes as reminders of the travels of their 18th-century relatives, and emblems of their cosmopolitan tastes. Inevitably, so successful an artist was also constantly copied and imitated by both English and lesser Italian painters throughout the 18th century. Although such works are desirable and sought after in their own right, they hardly compare in quality – and certainly not in price – to original works by Canaletto, which even in the early '80s could make many hundreds of thousands of pounds. Could these, then, be the real thing?

The photographs were too small to allow an exact assessment of quality but large enough to give an impression, which was helped when Mr Giovanini, the owner of the paintings, told Henry their actual size: 24 × 28 inches. Henry immediately asked if he could go and see them, but Mr Giovanini replied that it was not possible. (Henry later found out that they were with his father, a 91-year-old art dealer in Nijmegen in Holland.) He now felt a sudden fear that he might never see Mr Giovanini or the pictures again. 'It was like the feeling of losing a fish,' he recalled. 'I explained to him that they were potentially very interesting, but I had no way of pulling them in.' Henry took down further details of where and how Mr Giovanini could be contacted, asked if he could keep the photographs, and the next day returned to London in a mood of acute frustration. On arriving back at Christie's, one of his first stops was Charles Beddington. He dropped the photographs on his desk and told Charles of his meeting with Mr Giovanini. He had no earlier provenance for the pictures and asked Charles if he could turn his mind to establishing more of their history.

Fig. 33. Antonio Canaletto: *The Grand Canal*, looking north west from the Palazzo Corner to the Palazzo Contarini degli Scrigni.

455 ⦿

***After the Antique:* A Bronze Figure of a Faun, late 19th Century,** standing naked playing the cymbals, one foot raised on a pair of bellows, *rich green weathered patination, 79cm.; 31in. high*

£1,200–1,800

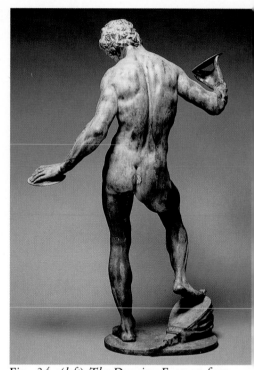

Fig. 34. (*left*) *The Dancing Faun* at first auction.

Figs. 35–7. *The Dancing Faun* by Adriaen de Vries (courtesy of Sotheby's).

Fig. 38. *The Dancing Faun* when in the Pearces' garden.

Fig. 39. Lord and Lady Pearce.

Fig. 40. The Gainsborough double portrait reunited, and also showing the remaining missing areas.

Fig. 41. *Sir Coutts Lindsay*, self-portrait.

Fig. 42. *Sir Coutts Lindsay* by Julia
Margaret Cameron. National Portrait
Gallery, London.

Fig. 45 (*above*) The Elsheimer Tabernacle now complete. Stadelsch Kunstinst.

Fig. 43. (*opposite, top*) The Adam Elsheimer Tabernacle with the two panels missing. Stadelsch Kunstinst.

Fig. 44. (*opposite, bottom*) A missing panel from the altarpiece. Stadelsch Kunstinst.

Fig. 46. (*overleaf*) Complete with frame, *The Fairy Fantasy* by John Anster Fitzgerald.

An auction department before catalogue deadline is as feverish as the news desk of a national newspaper. When the cut-off point for the next sale looms close, the condition of some cataloguers is occasionally physically and mentally diagnosable; the tyranny of having to find, photograph and fully catalogue two hundred lots with just days to go, can cause behaviour not unlike shell-shock. Not only are there the expectations of management, but the auction is a public show and judged by one's fellow staff, the trade, academics and the public, all of whom can be cruel critics. The illustrated catalogue is a widely published document and subject to the caustic scrutiny of competitors, the press and academic know-alls, all of whom derive considerable delight from pointing out errors. Consequently, the London auctioneer is a tough bird, and those who survive on the frontline of cataloguing are to be admired.

Charles, whose job was then specifically as a researcher, had a desk awash with paperwork. Believing firmly that a tidy desk is a sign of a limited mind, he was in the process of researching over twenty pictures and had books, articles and forms covering all available working space. Charles enjoys the pressure of deadlines, as do most journalists, but his most productive work tends to take place when everybody else has gone to bed, and the essential and constant demands of the day have ceased. He looks forward to the sanctuary of night when, freed from the noise and distractions of the day, he can turn his mind, unhurried and unbombarded, to the challenges before him.

At around ten o'clock Charles found Henry's photographs beneath a pile of others, and leant back in his chair to consider them, able for the first time that day to concentrate on a single subject. Apart from the odd security guard, he was alone in the cavernous building in King Street, and although hemmed in by burglar alarms (which allowed only one elaborate exit route, and occasional access to a loo), he relished his inaccessibility and solitude. The telephones had ceased their incessant interruption, the floor had cleared of secretaries and cataloguers, the endless meetings and appointments were long over, and he now allowed his mind to settle upon the images in front of him.

For the first stages of research, photographs can be a very useful guide. They give little conclusive indication of the physical properties of canvas and paint, but can impart the necessary information to study the composition. The composition, or subject, is something that can be easily copied by imitators or fakers, and is therefore only one part of the deduction process in attribution, but with these Polaroids Charles could at least form a view of whose work the paintings were meant to be taken for. Canaletto was an obvious possibility from the outset, so Charles reached for the authoritative tome on the subject, the *catalogue raisonné*, or complete listing of the artist's works, compiled by W. G. Constable. Most major painters' works are listed in this type of catalogue by art historians, with varying degrees of reliability, and they form the basis of any serious art library.

The photograph Charles studied first was a view of the Grand Canal looking north-east from the Palazzo Tiepolo towards the Rialto, and he fully expected to find the exact composition of which this was a copy amongst the paintings in the book. Slowly turning over each page of illustrations, after fifteen minutes he had reached the end but found no comparative oil painting. Instead he came across a written reference to a drawing of what appeared to be a similar subject in a different section of the book. Turning to an illustration of it, sure enough it showed, in bold black and white, the very same composition he held in his hand. The drawing had been executed, the author explained, by Canaletto's engraver Antonio Visentini, who was copying the composition into a slightly simplified form that could then be turned into a print. Famous artists used prints as a way of increasing their fame and also a source of easy revenue, and many of Canaletto's major works were reproduced in this way by his pet engraver, Visentini. What he read next caused Charles to sit up in his chair: 'No painting of this subject has been found; but that one exists or existed is indicated by [this] drawing.' Lights began to flash in his head. The picture was highly unlikely to be a modern copy, as there was no painting recorded from which it could have been done, and the drawing alone provided insufficient information to be used as the basis for a mocked-up or fake oil painting. This left only two likely alternatives: either that this was an early copy, done after a now lost original, or that this photograph showed none other than the lost original itself. He looked long and hard at the photo, trying to assess its detail and quality, but found it impossible to deduce more.

Charles then turned to the second of the two photographs. This was another view of the Grand Canal, but this time looking north-west from the Palazzo Corner to the Palazzo Contarini dagli Scrigni. Looking through the illustrations in Constable's catalogue, this time he was almost instantly faced with what looked like the same picture. The catalogue entry informed that it was a work in the collection of the Duke of Bedford at Woburn. Holding the photograph next to the illustration on the page, he intently scrutinised and compared the two images, centimetre by centimetre, starting with the architecture and then moving into the canal. What looked at first glance like exactly the same picture now appeared to have substantial differences in the water. A small boat towing a barge in the Woburn version was omitted from the picture in the photograph; the latter also had gondolas in different positions and a barge in front of the Palazzo Corner. The *coup de grâce* came next. In the catalogue entry for the picture, Constable pointed out that the Woburn version had been engraved by Visentini, but that he had arranged part of the composition differently, the described rearrangements corresponding exactly with the composition in Charles's hand. The inescapable conclusion to be drawn from this was that Visentini had not engraved the Woburn picture but *this* image, and that there were in fact two variants, both by Canaletto, of the same composition. In other words, Constable had wrongly speculated that the engraver had tampered with the Woburn composition, unaware that there was another composition which he was, in fact, slavishly following.

The weight of circumstantial evidence was now mounting almost conclusively in favour of these two compositions being by the master himself, works which had, for some reason, escaped the literature of art history. Certainty would not come until the paintings came to London and were examined in the flesh, but the likelihood that they were both copies of lost original works now seemed remote: better speculative evidence was difficult to imagine. Charles looked at his watch and saw that it was past eleven and time to go home, but before he left he rummaged through his desk and found the thickest red marker pen he could lay his hands on, and wrote in the largest writing a sheet of A4 would allow: 'Take a look at this – Charles.' He then propped it on Henry's desk, along with several photocopies, and went home to bed.

As with all auctioneers in the same situation, Henry was quite aware that if he gave too much away on the telephone to Mr Giovanini there was a danger that he might then take his paintings elsewhere. Now that Charles's research had firmly established their likely authenticity, the paintings had all but become outstandingly valuable objects. There was also a degree of academic prudence to be maintained, but Henry intimated to Mr Giovanini that the pictures could well be genuine. Not only Christie's, he told him, but a further expert – the British authority on Canaletto, J. G. Links – would need to see the paintings in order to give them a conclusive bill of health. They could then examine their condition also, a critical part of any commercial assessment, and come up with what they considered to be a fair auction estimate, should he be prepared to consign them for sale.

Although Mr Giovanini agreed to send the paintings over, Henry was still not convinced. Too often he had known pictures expected for sale, particularly exciting ones, to evaporate at the eleventh hour. He had also had to tell Mr Giovanini that it would be important to ascertain how long the pictures had been in South Africa – in accordance with South African law, an export permit is necessary for paintings 'generally accepted' to have been 'in the Republic of South Africa for longer than eighty years'.

It transpired that they had indeed been in South Africa for a very long time. The full story of these pictures was not in fact fully known till some months later when a South African magazine, *Living*, put a journalist on the case. Henry and Charles read the article later that year, and discovered the extraordinary saga and events surrounding the pictures' emergence and subsequent sale at a Cape Town auction house.

The story begins in the late nineteenth century with a young assistant to an English diamond dealer whose name was Lionel Phillips. Handling and sorting the stones for his London employer fired Phillips' imagination about their origin, and at the age of twenty he decided to leave England for South Africa, to seek work on the fields from which they came. It was a dreadful journey by ship, and an even worse trek on to Kimberley by mule wagon, taking him a month in all. The terrain was appalling, and the sand had been so thick at one point he had had to travel on foot. But once arrived, he quickly flourished in his new environment and over the next twenty years pioneered a highly successful gold-mining business, becoming a South African mining magnate of plutocratic proportions, and later awarded a knighthood by the British government. He entered South African politics, and as a member of the Reform Committee was involved in the famous Jameson Raid to topple the government in 1895, for which he was sentenced to death. The sentence was subsequently revised to a phenomenally high fine of £25,000, which he duly paid.

His great passion was art, and together with his wife Florrie he became not only a famous collector but a patron also, their endeavours acknowledged as formative in the founding of the Johannesburg Art Gallery. They kept their private collections in two houses, in Cape Town and Johannesburg, and chose only the finest works, assiduously advised by European experts of the day. After their death, the beneficiaries of the estate dispersed the collection in an enormous sale. Sir Lionel had died in 1936 at the age of 81, and his wife Florrie died four years later.

The collection included a pair of unsigned pictures said by the authorities of the time to be by Antonio Canaletto. At the auction following Florrie's death in 1940 these paintings were purchased by an anonymous buyer, as by Canaletto, for the substantial sum of one hundred guineas. The auction was a significant event in South African art history, being described by Ashbeys (who were to sell the pair of pictures again in 1984) as 'without doubt the most important collection to be disposed of in South Africa'. The sale lasted five days.

The buyer, whose identity is a well-guarded secret but whose family name was referred to as 'Simpson' by the press in 1985, then took the paintings back to his farm in Boland where he enjoyed them for six years. On his death he bequeathed them to his son. By the time his son decided to sell them in 1984, the perception of their importance as works of art had waned with the progress of time. They had been stored in his garage – there was no room for them in his house – and one morning in October 1984 he loaded them into the back of his truck together with sixteen other pictures, having been pestered by his wife to get rid of them, and drove into Cape Town to visit an 'expert', known for his understanding of antique art. Mr Simpson was unaware of the value of the pictures and the Venetian scenes, he recalled, were so dirty that his wife had had a go at them with 'Handy Andy' some time before. Whatever its properties as a cleaning agent, it had fortunately not left its mark, and the works were in near 'pristine' dirty state when he unloaded them from his combi to show the valuer.

saying: 'But if I communicated to the whole of Cape Town, the whole of Cape Town would want to buy the Canalettos.'

Unwittingly, it would appear, the very person to whom Basil Robinson had shown the pictures for an academic opinion had decided that she wanted to buy them for herself, and it seems she had done her best to deflate their value shortly before the sale by questioning their authenticity as oil paintings! In the event she was the underbidder, for by now Giovanini was so set on buying them, having allegedly had one in his office for a while, that '[he] had made up [his] mind that [he] was going to buy them'. At the sale, every time Suzanne Guicciarde bid, she was topped by Giovanini, who ended up securing the pictures for R5,500 (£1,100). There was apparently one other bidder, the wife of a Johannesburg art dealer, but the rest of the room remained uncommitted for a pair of paintings that had been publicly doubted by the auctioneer, and were now selling for more than two and a half times their upper estimate.

It is difficult to fathom fully the story of the sale of these pictures first time round, with all the recriminations and face-saving that inevitably follow the sale of a sleeper. This had more than its fair share of unorthodox practice and farce, and the dramatic irony is that these two pictures had been sold by the same auction house forty-five years earlier for a hundred guineas, as part of probably the most celebrated collection in South African art history, and as fully authentic works by Canaletto, yet to which there was no reference in the 1984 catalogue. This, how-ever, may well have been due to nothing more than the passage of time.

* * *

After Henry had endured an 'awful two-month hiatus' after his telephone call to Mr Giovanini, the pictures mercifully arrived. Charles followed Henry down into the basement of King Street, passing the acres of racks upon which were stacked hundreds of pictures waiting to be lotted up and sold. The Venetian views had been delivered the previous evening and this was their first opportunity to view them for real. There was therefore the normal, mild professional trepidation in Henry and Charles's minds as they rounded the last corner of the subterranean maze, a defence mechanism that prevents the undue flow of adrenalin and elation until the last stage of the attribution process has been secured. As they neared the bench, Charles recalls thinking that he knew exactly what he wanted the paintings to look like. By this time he had developed an extremely well defined mental picture of them, drawn from his knowledge of other works by Canaletto.

On encountering a truly great work of art, with which you have become emotionally involved in the process of research, a work that then does not disappoint in any way, but fulfils and exceeds your expectations when finally viewed, the effect can be numinous. Every cell in your body is charged with excitement and admiration. Canaletto is an outstanding technician, and although his works lack the emotional intensity of a great Renaissance painter, those subjects he chose to exploit – the light effects, details of architecture, people at work and on water –particularly in his Venetian views, are carried off with such precise draughtsmanship, sureness of touch and sense of colour and grace, that they can fell you with their virtuosity. Henry and Charles were both struck at once by the pair's undoubtable authenticity, and as they gazed silently upon the two works, propped somewhat irreverently upon the carpenter's bench, neither of them felt inclined to say anything (*Figs. 32 & 33*).

The works were dirty, the varnish layer discoloured by grime, and although this did not altogether hide the colours, a small cleaning test in the top right-hand corner of one of them indicated a radiantly blue sky waiting to be revealed. Neither Charles nor Henry knew when or where this test had been done, but at some point in their recent history, possibly at the restorer's in

Cape Town, someone had opened up a window by removing the dirty varnish and thereby hinting to a prospective buyer the treasures that awaited. Having asked the British expert on Canaletto, J. G. Links, for the final authentication which is expected before offering any works by the artist in Britain, which was granted unreservedly and enthusiastically, Henry was then able to ring Mr Giovanini with the good news and discuss estimates. Christie's had an important old-master sale scheduled three months later in July, and after taking Henry's view, and comparing recent prices for the artist at auction, Giovanini agreed to a guide price of £120,000–£160,000 for each. Although these works were not necessarily conceived as a pair, or 'pendants', auction houses often recommend separating pairs of pictures as the sum of each sold independently is often greater than that achieved by selling them together, which can present too expensive a prospect to some buyers. The Canalettos were therefore duly illustrated in full-page colour as Lots 60 and 61 in Christie's major summer sale.

I have been unable to locate Mr Giovanini for his account of the day's sale, but a perfunctory version of the events as described by him was given in *Living* magazine.

Mr Giovanini and his wife flew from Africa for the sale, and on entering the crowded auction room on the morning of 5th July, found that there was nowhere for them to sit. A member of Christie's staff finally found them two seats, and after what 'seemed like an eternity', Lots 60 and 61 'were held aloft'. The bidding was instantly fierce from both the room with its assembly of dealers, and the telephones on behalf of international buyers. Henry was in the room, acting on behalf of what appeared to be the most determined buyer of all: although unknown to the room at the time, he was bidding for one of the leading American dealers, Hirschl and Adler. All the time their representative had a pen held to his mouth Henry was to keep on bidding, which he duly did, securing the first picture for the then phenomenal amount of £388,800 and giving Mr Giovanini a lump in his throat. The second Canaletto, with the view of the Rialto Bridge, went to the same buyer for slightly less at £345,600. That night, we are told, Mr Giovanini and his wife celebrated in a French restaurant on Oxford Street with 'real French champagne' and have not been heard of by Christie's since. The funds, in accordance with the law, went back to South Africa.

For Charles it was tangible proof that his late-night sessions bear fruit. Ten years on, he is still with Christie's, although recently moved to New York. He has sustained his reputation for diligent cataloguing, and also continues a personal crusade to out, and awaken, any potential sleeper that may pass before him.

After a short spell as an independent dealer, Henry Wyndham has gone on to become the UK Chairman of Sotheby's.

CHAPTER EIGHT

The Mystery of
The Dancing Faun

NO DEALER AROUND at the time will ever forget the momentous happenings at Sotheby's on the morning of 7th December 1989. On that day a 32-inch-high bronze Renaissance sculpture of a dancing faun broke all auction records and made £6.82 million; unbelievably, six months earlier, the same piece of sculpture had been rescued from Sotheby's sale of garden statuary in Sussex, where it was about to be sold as a 19th-century copy after the antique, with an estimate of £1,200–£1,800.

Both the British and American press reacted with bemused awe. *Today* newspaper announced, 'SEVEN MILLION FOR A GARDEN GNOME'; the *San Francisco Chronicle* headlined 'A GEM FROM A GARDEN', while the quality British dailies ran large, front-page illustrations of the bronze figure with spirited reports of the auction. For the cartoonists it was a gift: Pozzi in the *People* illustrated a line of hopeful vendors, garden gnomes in hand, queuing up at the counter of Sotheby's; and in the *Mail on Sunday* Jak showed an old couple listening to the proprietor of a garden centre, with the caption: 'When we saw how much

the last one went for, we stopped making garden gnomes.'
Behind him was a mass of priced-up, dancing plaster fauns.

Yet despite all their fervour, the reporters were frustrated by
a vital piece of missing information which would have made their
story complete: the name of, or at least a reaction from, the
person who sold the faun. This did not prevent fabrication. In
a style later found in coverage of the Lottery, *The Times* and
Telegraph described the anonymous vendor as an 'elderly couple',
the *Daily Mail* said that they were 'absolutely thrilled' and the
Sun that they were 'reported to be speechless'. This was fiction,
however. Sotheby's had steadfastly preserved the anonymity of
their client, and their client had remained silent.

For a short time, not only the media but the art world too
were fascinated by the sculpture's extraordinary provenance. In
advance of newspaper reports, accounts of the morning's events
flowed down Bond Street like an over-running bath, reaching
even the most inaccessible West End dealers by close of business
that day. I remember first being told by a restorer in his studio
in neighbouring Albemarle Street, shortly after lunch, and
reacting like most others in the trade, with disbelief. For the
West End art trade it had the added piquancy of an item that,
had it not been withdrawn from the garden sale at the last
moment, they themselves could feasibly have bought for the price
of an unexciting old-master drawing, or a mediocre Victorian
landscape. Few also could help but try and imagine what it must
have been like to be the witless vendor, who had presumably
regarded the Dancing Faun as little more than a glorified bird
perch for the last forty years, and had now just witnessed its
sale, before an astounded art world, for a little under seven
million pounds, including the buyer's premium. But it was difficult to identify with the owner: no one had a proper clue as to
his or her identity, and the imagination needed more to cling
to.

The story deserved more space, but the papers had little to

go on. The *Telegraph*'s front page used a quote from an unattributed source that the sellers were 'ordinary people' from Brighton, and proceeded to explain, using the sparse known facts, that the sculpture had originally been destined for a sale of garden statuary in Sussex, and had been pulled out at the eleventh hour by Elizabeth Wilson, Sotheby's sculpture expert in Bond Street, who had recognised its previously unseen qualities. The *Sun* gave the story more colour by adding that the sculpture had been 'collecting grime and green mould for more than thirty years since the couple paid £100 for it and stood it in their garden'. The *Guardian*, with others, moved to safer ground with an extensive quote from the purchaser, a distinguished West End sculpture dealer: 'In my thirty-five years of dealing, this is the greatest sculpture that has ever come to the market!' he exclaimed, and went on to extol the virtues of the sculptor, Adriaen de Vries. (A cynical reporter might have added that, having paid £7 million, and faced now with the job of moving it on for a profit, he *would* say that. He had beaten the last record for a bronze at auction by £1.7 million, and this has still not been bettered!)

By the following week the euphoria had subsided, but the mystery remained. The lucky seller's identity became a padlocked commercial secret – one of the thousands of vigilantly guarded names of vendors held within all the major auction houses, and known only to a very select few. And so it remained for five years. Until, that is, I was six months into writing this book and received a telephone call from an art dealer I had not encountered before. It was a weekday morning in June 1994, and I was at my gallery in Bond Street.

'My name is Nick Bowlby,' the caller said, 'and I think I might have something that could be useful for your book.' The discussion went little further than that intriguing introduction before we arranged to meet when he was next in London.

I made some enquiries about Mr Bowlby through a couple of other dealers, who told me that for the last fifteen years Bowlby, an art dealer of about forty, had been selling 19th- and 20th-century British watercolours and paintings, not from London, but from a gallery in Tunbridge Wells. Those who knew him liked his natural but professional style, his easy manner and enthusiasm.

Soon after arriving at my office Nick Bowlby brought up the subject of his telephone call again. The person who had sold the Dancing Faun, he explained, had had an enormous impact on his life, not just as the owner of a record-breaking discovery, but as a human being. 'There are two or three people who have a profound effect on you,' he said, 'and he was one of them. It's true to say that I adored him.' He told me that the owner had intended to make the story public on his own terms but, becoming ill and sensing the end, had asked Nicholas to do it on his behalf. After his death, the owner's family then felt they weren't ready for the attention, and so put it off. Although since then Nicholas had considered various ways of presenting the story, he had resisted making recommendations to the family, partly, one suspects, for the lack of an appropriate stage. Now, five years later, and with this book, it seemed he might have found one.

Without giving too much away, Nick explained that he had originally become acquainted with the owner of the Faun through his son, who was Nick's friend and lived close by. The friend's father was an artist and collector, and Nick was enrolled to help exhibit and sell his works. But early on in their dealings Nick became captivated by the old man's formidable charm, establishing a friendship which culminated in visits two or three times a week towards the end of his life, and out of which came the Dancing Faun. The quality of Nick's friendship and regard for the old man had evidently run very deep, and seemed as great, if not greater, than that of a son for a father.

This was as much as Nick was prepared to tell me at this first meeting. To continue he would need first to go to the family for approval. As he had talked about the vendor, his speech had quickened, both his words and manner expressing a profound desire to fulfil his friend's wishes, and for whom, posthumously, he was now acting as spokesman. Although I tried to ask more questions, Nick insisted that we wait until our next meeting and, assuring me that I would hear from him shortly, left me waiting at the gallery door for more.

It took Nick longer than I hoped, but finally, three days later, he rang to say that the family had given him the all-clear, and I hurriedly fixed a further appointment for the following week. Anticipating a successful outcome, I had, in fact, been asking around in the art world about the Dancing Faun. Almost without exception it was remembered by all, and my questions were met with smiles of recollection as well as curiosity about the identity of the astonishingly fortunate 'old couple'. Now that the family had given me the go-ahead, I rang Liz Wilson at Sotheby's, explained the situation, and two days later was able to meet her to hear her account of the discovery.

Miss Elizabeth Wilson, a main-board director, had been working at Sotheby's for thirty-five years, and the de Vries discovery, together with many others, had enhanced her reputation for knowledge and connoisseurship. She is one of the doyennes of the auction world, famed for her sustained commitment and industry, working zealously in the compilation of her sale catalogues and noted for her indifference to public recognition and all that it involves. Her reputation also extends far abroad; she travels incessantly and earlier in the year had spent two months in California on a Getty study award, adding to her knowledge of early-European sculpture.

Liz Wilson recounted the story from the beginning. It was a weekday in the summer of 1989, and she had arranged to meet a friend for lunch in a restaurant popular with the art world called The Chalet in Grosvenor Street. As she left her nearby Bond Street office, she picked up from the front counter one of Sotheby's own recently produced garden statuary catalogues. It was still a boom-time for art dealers, almost everything seemed to be selling, and the major auction houses had now resorted to looking into people's back gardens for fresh stock. Garden ornaments such as stone and cast-metal Victorian seats, birds, mammals, and figures, which had formerly been deemed second-ary antiques of low status, were now making thousands of pounds, while more noble stone and bronze sculpture, or garden gates, could achieve anything up to £100,000. This was a new market for both Sotheby's and Christie's, who had decided that they too could capitalise on the prodigious prices for which such items were now changing hands. Although not her specific department, as Head of Works of Art Liz took it upon herself to keep an eye on these sales to make sure that no obvious high-quality collectors' or museum pieces slipped by as garden furniture or bird-baths. She had already been down to Sotheby's Sussex auction rooms, where the sales are held, for an early viewing the previous week to check for any sleepers, but this was her first chance to study the illustrated catalogue – the second stage of the checking procedure which she regarded as 'one of those jobs that has to be done'. While waiting for her friend to arrive, she began flipping through the catalogue, and remembers noticing a preponderance of garden seats and wondering whether these were an entirely appropriate subject for Sotheby's, the 'Fine Art Auctioneers'.

Some months earlier, in her peregrinations around Europe, Liz had been to Prague for an exhibition of sculpture produced in the region around 1600, and had been enthralled by the genius of one particular sculptor, who appeared far and away to outshine his contemporaries. His name was Adriaen de Vries. Until that time, she says, she had not fully realised 'what a giant he was' artistically, and partly attributed this to the scarcity of his bronze sculptures, most of which are in Sweden and many of which were Imperial commissions from Emperor Rudolf II. Unlike the creations of many of his predecessors and contemporaries, de Vries never repeated his sculptures in multiple castings: the terracotta mould remained inside the bronze, preventing duplication by himself or others. Perhaps because they were mostly Imperial commissions, each of his creations remained a one-off, the exclusive property of his auspicious client and unavailable to other European collectors. As a result, de Vries's work is little known either on the open market or to museums, and the exhibition, with its many examples, proved a thrilling revelation and one she could not forget.

There is a synchronistic phenomenon that I have experienced with many art discoveries: when new interest in and knowledge of an artist waylay you, rather like a new word learned, there is a high likelihood of coming across them again shortly afterwards. In a strange way, it is almost as if the regard you have felt for something or someone summons them into your presence. And so it was that as the garden seats gave way to urns, and urns to fireplaces, Liz came to the section on bronze and marble statuary; she took a closer interest here because it fell more directly into her area of expertise and, carefully studying the photographs, she came upon it (*Fig. 34*). It was illustrated in black and white between a bronze naked maiden and a seated nymph, and simply catalogued as, 'After the Antique: A Bronze figure of a faun, late 19th century . . .' with an estimate of £1,200–£1,800. Liz had not seen the piece when she had been in Sussex the previous week – it must have been in storage – but even in black-and-white the image now hit her with astounding force. Not even its ignominious setting amongst garden ornaments could detract from her immediate realisation that this had to be a masterwork by her new 'giant', Adriaen de Vries. To be one hundred per cent sure, she would need to see it.

As soon as she could get back from lunch, Liz telephoned the company's Sussex office and was connected to Jen Cox, a young secretary in the garden statuary department. Trying to sound calm, she asked Jen to put the garden statue aside so that she could drive down to inspect it the following morning before work. But she was unable to conceal her excitement, and her fervent tone gave her away. 'Good Heavens,' said Jen, and promptly volunteered to put it in her car and drive it up to Bond Street that evening. 'She was so brilliant,' Liz recalls, 'and I thankfully accepted.' She asked for the figure to be dropped off at the office, so that she could return after hours and inspect it that very night.

* * *

Liz entered the front door of Sotheby's at 9pm, bade good evening to the security guards, and walked straight to a locked office on the ground floor. Trying to key in the code to the door, she found herself unable to recall the numbers. After a series of failed attempts she drew a deep breath and tried again. This time it worked. The lock clicked and she turned the handle, opening the door into an unlit office. Through the gloom she began to make out the shape of a human torso, with arms outsplayed, its barely discernible bronze surface a dead, black gleam. Her excitement grew as the form gained greater coherence, its facial features and muscular contortions becoming readable in the darkness. She then turned on the light. The figure was naked, save for a partial mantle of coloured corrosion — a green, oxidised surface which reassuringly testified to the piece's antiquity as well as the long years it had spent outdoors. She was presented with an athlete in the act of juggling two plates (not cymbals as the catalogue had stated), his head tilted downwards, his body complexly balanced, and under his right foot a pair of bellows. An enraptured American art historian later described it as a 'virtuoso exercise in the depiction of dynamic equilibrium'. The electric light brought out even more to delight her eye: every inch of the sculpture's surface seemed to pulsate with life. In getting on for twenty-five years she could not remember anything as beautiful as this coming through the doors. Being, she admits, of a superstitious nature, she then went to her drawer, took out a pen and paper, and left a small note propped against the base – 'De Vries was here'. If she did not make it through the night, she reflected, then at least someone could carry on where she had left off. She then closed the door and went home to a sleepless night.

'The next day,' she continued, 'the rest of the department gathered round to see it. We had a window above us that lit it naturally. It was the perfect way to view it. I genuinely believe, thinking back to that morning, that it never looked more marvellous than then.' She looked down for a moment, to further recollect the sensation, and then smiled: 'It was in motion, you know . . . it really seemed to move!'

A few days later Liz invited an art historian from one of the national museums who specialises in this area of mannerist sculpture and who endorsed the attribution to de Vries unreservedly. Although I can imagine it, it is difficult to describe what it was that originally communicated itself to Liz with such certainty from the garden catalogue. It is perhaps sufficient to say that if you have spent thirty years examining photographs, book illustrations, the objects themselves, the fakes and the reproductions, forever addressing the question all cataloguers constantly ask about what it is that differentiates the real thing from the comparatively worthless copy, and doing so with the speed and efficiency that the sales process requires, an intelligent person cannot help but hone their perceptions. We can assume that Liz had seen enough sculpture and works of art from the Renaissance onwards to know the seminal images from which copies and reproductions spring. Sculptors of the Renaissance would often use classical sculptures as their starting point, adding their own interpretation to early Roman and Greek prototypes, to which they gained access in the collections of the Pope or contemporary European princes. Liz would have recognised the sculpture as a unique adaptation of a marble Roman faun now housed in the

Tribuna of the Uffizi in Florence. But the sculptor, conforming to the mannerist style, which attempted to enhance sculpture with drama and emotion, eliminated the horns and small tail found on the marble original, transformed the cymbals it was carrying into plates for juggling, and together with outstanding refinement to the anatomy, turned the Faun into an object of immeasurable human grace (to be pedantic, therefore, he was now no longer a faun, but an acrobat!). As a further, rather odd, adaptation from the classical original, a foot-accordion under the leg of the faun had either been misread, or changed in the interpretation for a pair of bellows. The other sculptural adaptations of this subject, which Liz would most likely have come across, would have dated from the late 17th century onwards – not the late-16th- and early-17th-century mannerist period, which the style of *this* evoked. Unfamiliar and artistically sublime, it fitted perfectly into what she now knew of de Vries's exceptional body of work.

But looking at the garden-sale catalogue, it is also possible to see how Liz would have more than a purely intellectual reaction to the black-and-white image. As most art historians will tell you, a monochrome photograph is often more useful than a colour one for assessing the technique and quality of a work of art. Despite, or rather because of the lack of colour, it can portray tonal range and detail more precisely and clinically, and therefore informatively, than a more decorative colour photograph. Even in the small catalogue illustration, the sublime skill with which de Vries shaped the muscles of the acrobat's thighs and torso, and the tresses and curls in his hair, makes all the other black-and-white images in the catalogue look like plaster fairings by comparison. Interestingly, however, when Sotheby's photographer, John Quinn, was summoned by the department the following week to take a definitive photograph of the discovery, he felt defeated by the challenge. Liz put it down to the definition of a great three-dimensional work of art, but however he placed it, in varying lights, angles and backgrounds, he found himself quite incapable of recording its phenomenal subtlety and poise. After a month of trying he gave up and settled for his best attempt: the Faun's extraordinary poise and beauty literally went beyond the powers of an expert photographer, with state-of-the-art equipment (*Figs. 35, 36 & 37*).

'I then sweated,' Liz recalled, 'for now came the waiting. It is standard to do a thermoluminescent test for these things to establish the date, so we sent it to the Oxford Research Laboratory.' Rather like carbon-dating, this is a highly technical scientific process which can establish the approximate period of an object (providing it is of a testable material), and thereby help endorse the judgement reached separately by art-historical means. The sculpture's outer metal was not testable, but its inner terracotta core was as it contained readable levels of natural uranium. Liz was now obliged to wait for two weeks for the test results. 'I did not doubt the Faun's date, but you never know what these scientific analyses can come up with,' she told me. 'The days dragged by.' After what must have felt to Liz like a cruel delay, she received the telephone call: the terracotta core was found to have been fired between 540 and 360 years ago and therefore easily within de Vries's lifetime. It was the news she had been waiting for.

It was now up to Liz to decide what the Faun was worth. The only other occasion that a de Vries had come up at auction in recent times was five years before in Paris. It was a bronze of a rearing horse, but barely compared in quality to the dynamic Faun, and had made just over a million dollars, ending up in the Getty Museum in California. But the Faun's sale estimate was something she would also have to discuss with the owner. And as soon as it had been withdrawn from the Sussex sale she had, in fact, rung Nick Bowlby, who was acting as agent for the vendor. He, in turn, had delivered the news to his friend.

* * *

I was very much looking forward to my next meeting with Nick Bowlby. The story of the Faun had fascinated me, particularly now that I had the prospect of being amongst the first to relate the identity of the Faun's owner to the world at large. Nick was considerably more relaxed at our second interview. He had spoken to the family, they were keen to go ahead, and my dictaphone was running. 'So shall we start from the beginning,' I began 'with this elderly couple from Brighton whom the newspapers referred to?'

'I don't know where they got Brighton from,' Nick replied. 'It wasn't a couple either, but a single widowed man.' I waited expectantly through the pause that followed. 'The sale of the Faun was one of the last events in the life of an extraordinary man.' Slightly reluctantly, I thought, he then produced a huge wedge of newspaper obituaries from his black file. 'I think it will surprise people,' he continued, 'when they hear he was one of the most senior Law Lords in the country.' He unfolded some of the larger cuttings and placed them in front of me. 'His name was Lord Pearce.'

And so it was that one of the better-kept secrets of the art world was revealed, not as an indiscretion, but at the behest of the owner himself, and four years after his death.

Edward Holroyd Pearce, Lord of Appeal in Ordinary, was the son of a prep-school teacher, read Classics at Oxford where he was a Scholar, and in 1925 was called to the Bar at Lincoln's Inn. His career continued in a sharply vertical direction. He acquired a flourishing practice, taking silk in 1945, and three years later was made a High Court judge, culminating in the position of Lord of Appeal between 1962 and 1967. His later public roles included the successful heading-up of the commission into the future of Rhodesia and chairman-ship of the Press Council. If I wanted more biography, Nick told me, I could read it all in detail in the obituaries, but for the time being, rather than tell me about the meritocrat, he was keen to talk about the private man, whom he knew better.

As a young barrister, Pearce contracted TB and this, Nick told me, was something kept from his contemporaries. He was so ill that his chosen profession was deemed too demanding for his frail constitution, and the doctors feared for his life should he continue. At the time he was living in a flat up a hundred stairs in Lincoln's Inn, making the pursuit of his career all the more arduous. But with steely resolve, and practical resourcefulness, he managed to establish a *modus vivendi* to which he then strenuously adhered, but which also set certain limits on his life. The doctors' orders were draconian: he was to have breakfast in bed, rising only at the last moment; at lunchtime he was to return home to rest, and should always eat something; in the evening he was to retire to bed for supper, and parties or any sort of night life were absolutely banned. Although to the outside world he appeared a thrusting, career-building barrister, at home he was a virtual invalid. He continued this routine all his life, and although his behaviour may have appeared antisocial or even agoraphobic to those who did not know him well (and he rarely if ever talked about his illness), he remained alive, relying heavily on the sustenance of his home and family.

Most prominent in this way of life was his outstanding wife (*Fig. 39*). In 1927 Pearce married Erica, the second daughter of the early-20th-century artist, Bertram Priestman RA. The Priestmans were of Suffolk Quaker origin, and Erica's 'quiet, understated good humour acted as a backdrop', Nicholas recalled, 'to her husband's firework displays.' Their devotion to each other was obvious till the end, and Nick attributed a large part of Pearce's success to Erica's constant allegiance. They had two sons, both of whom followed their father into Law.

They lived at a place called Gyll Farm, in Crowborough, partly on the advice of their doctor, who recommended that they move to an area near Tunbridge Wells, historically prized for its healing environment. 'Try Crowborough,' he added, so they did, and their search took them on a walk down a lane skirting a golf course. As a site for a house it was exquisite, being high enough to survey a major part of the Weald of Kent and the South Downs, and adjoined on one side by the protecting presence of Ashdown Forest. A plot of land was available for sale so they bought it, built a house from scratch, and fenced off a large garden which absorbed much of their joint creativity and time for the next fifty years. Shortly after Erica died, predeceasing Edward by four years, he and Nicholas and Nicholas's wife Rosalind collated and edited a manuscript which Erica had written on the creation of her garden, and published it as a charming book entitled *The Permissive Garden*.

In the first chapter she asks whether readers would like to see the garden, and then goes on to describe it. 'It stands five hundred feet up adjoining a gorse- and bracken-covered common. It is surrounded by hedges of holly, oak, beech, cypress, laurel, hazel, yew, birch, brambles – in fact the old country hedge. The extent of the land is about one and a third acres.' 'You didn't know you were entering the garden until you were in,' Nicholas recalled. 'And then it was a labyrinth of paths and little surprises.'

'If you have any urns or stone ornaments around, I think they do enhance a garden,' Erica wrote, and their own garden was exemplary in this respect. Around corners, next to bushes, beside and in water there were at least forty pieces of sculpture. 'You had to walk to find them,' Nicholas told me, 'but then you chanced upon them.' Many were classical sculptures of gods and nymphs, but there were also Japanese storm-lanterns and lead water-tanks, either set on plinths or resting against walls. In a paved garden without lawns, it was an ideal aesthetic solution for the two artists, and they exploited the idea fully, making sure that all the pieces were tastefully integrated. Counted amongst them, and not even in a particularly prominent position, set upon a white stone base that stood amongst lavender and was bordered by a tall privet, dwelt the Dancing Faun (*Fig. 38*). Together with most of the other ornaments in the garden, it had been bought in the '40s or '50s at Christie's between Edward Pearce's trips to and from the law courts. At the time he was a judge and just beginning to achieve prominence, and a deep affection for home made him open to anything of beauty that he could afford for his house and garden. This included carpets, paintings and furniture, but he rarely spent more than £20 on any object. He bought the Dancing Faun together with some other ornaments, in a 'job lot' consigned from France (no earlier provenance for the sculpture has been found), for seven guineas in 1951. This was not a particularly surprising price for the period. Even if the Faun had been fully catalogued as by de Vries, neither scholarship nor the market were sufficiently evolved to react euphorically to an outstanding bronze. In the '50s there was little demand for even the best Renaissance sculpture, and it was possible to go home with a reasonable work by the greatest practitioners, such as Jan Bologna (de Vries's master) for under £500. The price of seven guineas for an unattributed bronze of this beauty was still paltry, but not sensationally so for 1951.

The Dancing Faun was therefore perhaps closer to being a 'garden gnome' than the tabloids would have dared hope. It was bought as decoration, as an attractive but not overly expensive 'eye-catcher' in a garden that became the canvas for a private and loving relationship. The garden statuary was the equivalent of details in a jointly conceived and executed work of art which the two artists created for their own benefit. The Faun's commercial value was therefore neither rated nor important for the role which it fulfilled in the mythological and human tableaux that the pair staged in their private garden.

'Erica's heart broke at the death of her second son in 1985.' Her two children lived nearby and regularly visited their parents. Both were barristers and the eldest, Bruce, went on to become a well-known High Court judge himself. But neither had the fortune of their father when it came to fending off illness, and the two brothers, the second three years after the first, both died of brain tumours. For their father the terrible blow was doubled by the death in 1987 of Erica who had been greatly weakened by the death of her second son, two years earlier.

Edward found a way of relieving his sadness by directing his energies into publishing the manuscript of Erica's book. With Pearce in editorial control, and the publishing expertise provided by Nick and Rosalind, who was an experienced editor, the project took shape on the Bowlbys' kitchen table after their children had gone to bed at night. 'Pearce was a realist,' Nick recalled. 'He wanted to produce a book which was also a commercial success. He had a very sound business approach, and had even managed to help educate his children with the sale of a local wireless company which he had founded himself as a young man. He was a very practical man.'

The book was published to great critical acclaim. Pearce relished the publicity, and was even interviewed on television in his garden. 'It had a rejuvenating effect. He loved all the attention and activity, particularly as it centred on Erica.' It was also a great pleasure for Nick to see his friend happy after so much bereavement.

But the publicity brought with it a sinister element. The police came to Pearce with the information that a burglar, drawn by the publicity, was planning to steal some of the statues. They had been tipped off that he was due the following week and likely to be armed, so the old man, now 88, stayed with one of his daughters-in-law on the night in question, and the police lay in wait. This happened twice, but the burglar did not show up. The experience, however, was enough to persuade Pearce that the sculptures were a liability, and after discussing the matter with Nick, reluctantly asked him to dispose of them.

'Seeing them all loaded up into the van for Sotheby's was like watching prizes on *The Generation Game*,' Nick recalled. He hadn't realised how many there were, and the forty or so pieces filled a lorry. The Faun was just one of many. Despite the humour in his recollection, however, it was a sad sight for Nick who felt strongly for the old man having to watch the dismantling of so cherished a part of his life. The pieces were then driven to Sotheby's Billingshurst to be lotted up. Some of the lesser items, such as 19th-century copper jardinières and turn-of-the-century stone ornaments were estimated in the low hundreds, but a number of the more distinguished objects, including the Faun, were expected to achieve low thousands in the new and buoyant garden-furniture market. They were entered into two sales, and at the time the Faun was not considered as commercial as some of the other larger works. Some of the decorative works did later achieve prices in the low thousands.

It is easy to see how a garden-statuary expert, with his eye tuned in to garden seats and gates, would not have dwelt long on assessing the commercial quality of the Dancing Faun. Not only was it relatively small (31 inches high) and therefore of less importance in landscaping terms than a lot of the other exhibits, but bronze, like other metals, is exceedingly difficult to date, particularly when weathered, and lacks the sure indications of age that are normally found in, say, a work of oil on canvas or a textile. In any event, patination can be easily faked by an expert forger, leading to still less confidence amongst non-specialists. Even an expert on the subject can have difficulties persuading the world at large of an object's age, which was why the thermo-luminescent test that Liz Wilson had done in Oxford was so important to corroborate her discovery.

'I went to see Pearce when Liz telephoned me with the news of her find,' Nick told me. 'He was extremely pleased and inter-ested, but it would be inaccurate to describe him as overly excited. He was too old and worldly, he had seen too much of life to be enormously affected.' None the less, he was keen to be kept abreast of every development from there on. Although not a rich man, he had made himself comfortably off with a combination of a judge's salary and his small-scale local business ventures. He pragmatically viewed the money he was likely to receive from the Faun – estimated at £1.0–£1.5 million – as the means to make some property investments, but not as life-changing. Indeed, it was not altogether surprising to him that the magic, secret garden he and Erica had created with so much love and joint endeavour had yielded a fruit. There can be little doubt that, together with the loss of the children, he missed his wife terribly, and his garden existed as a proud and lasting testament of the inextinguishable love they bore for each other, a place of enduring enchantment in lonely old age. The emergence of a priceless object from its winding paths was not so strange, or unexpected, for a plot invested with such sentiment.

* * *

Apart from the price estimate, you can quickly gain a feeling for the regard an auction house has for an object by its 'packaging' in the catalogue. In the case of the de Vries Dancing Faun there was as much fanfare and red carpet as the traditional format would tastefully allow. The title of the sale on the front of the catalogue, 'European Works of Art and Sculpture', was specially extended to include the words 'The Dancing Faun by Adriaen de Vries'; the write-up inside had the density of a scholarly magazine article, with an unfolding, 24-inch-long illustration sheet showing the sculpture from three angles in full colour; the voluminous cataloguing also included a black-and-white detail of the arm, and a full biography of the sculptor in a 'heavy sell' reserved exclusively for items of outstanding significance and value. The public reaction was just as extraordinary. Liz Wilson recalled that it was the first time she could remember non-art-world people coming off the street, excitedly drawn to view the amazing object found in a back garden. 'Everyone who saw it was bowled over by its beauty. I had never known one of our works of art create such interest.'

So many onlookers arrived on the morning of the sale that there was no room for Nick Bowlby in the auction room, and he was obliged to stand in the next room where a loudspeaker transmitted the sale. Lord Pearce remained at home, close to the telephone, but one of his daughters-in-law, Julia, and three of the grandchildren, the oldest in his early twenties, took their places in reserved seats in the room. Television cameras and hungry journalists added to the throng, and one intrepid reporter, shrewdly speculating that one of the grandchildren was a possible relation of the Faun's vendor, later followed him to the gentleman's loos in a vain attempt to draw out his true identity. Taking the sale was George Hughes-Hartman, an experienced auctioneer, with Liz Wilson standing close by, keeping an eye open for the likely buyers, and her fingers crossed.

With great foresight, Nick had brought a tape-recorder with him to the sale, and he now produced the tape for me to hear. As he recorded the event by holding his machine up to the loudspeaker, it is possible to offer a word-for-word report of the phenomenal seven-minute match.

The bidding opened at £400,000. This was a mere formality, and at increments of £100,000 a time, the price rapidly escalated to £2 million. By £2.4 million the auctioneer's voice had become more serious and deliberate, his pauses longer, but the steady momentum was maintained. On the receipt of £2.6 million a sneeze echoed through the room, perhaps out of surprise, for the price had just doubled the higher estimate and there appeared to be two bidders resolutely locked in heavy combat. At around £3.5 million the pace slowed, but rarely to more than ten seconds between each increment, and thus the two bidders continued with steady and relentless intent. Each time Hughes-Hartman notched up another million you could hear the relief and achievement in his voice, as if he were counting press-ups, and he would begin again with renewed vigour. On the fifth of these he then increased the size of the bids to £200,000 a time. And yet still the two combatants fought on. They had now beaten the world record for a bronze, and the price was continuing upwards.

Looking for the next increment of £200,000, Hughes-Hartman called out for £5.6 million, and the voice of one of the bidders then broke the rhythm by offering £5.5 million instead, in what is known as 'splitting the bid'. It gave the impression of weakness, a would-be purchaser's last try, his absolute limit, and when the other buyer capped it with £5.7 million, Hughes-Hartman, perhaps to relieve his own and the room's incredulity, reacted prematurely. With the words 'to the man on the left against the telephone' (i.e. underbid by the telephone bidder), he slapped down the gavel. But the contest was not over, and after a brief kerfuffle he was obliged to let it reopen – the telephone bidder was still in the game. But the phone bidder's offering was little more than a death-throe. At £6.2 million the man in the room – his identity unknown to Nick who was still next door – delivered the final blow. With a more prudent delay this time between the words 'against him on the telephone' and the strike of the gavel, Hughes-Hartman then knocked it down to the man in the room, together with the 10 per cent buyer's premium, for a total price of £6.82 million.

The buyer was an eminent sculpture dealer from Bond Street called Cyril Humphris, who retired from business in 1995. It was an enormous and risky price for him to pay, but he believed the Faun to be the most important sculpture to come on the market since he started dealing, and one he had to secure at all costs. He later vindicated his judgement by selling it on to the Getty Foundation in California for an undisclosed price, but which was rumoured to be not greatly in excess of the final bid. The underbidder on the telephone has not been named.

Lord Pearce died barely a year after the sale of the de Vries and was unable to fulfil his schemes to speculate with the money.

'It was a great pity,' Nick said. 'He had some very specific plans.'

'But how did he react when he heard that the Faun made so much?' I asked. The second side of my tape had come to an end, and by now so had Nick and his story.

'I rang him from the auction house minutes after it sold and told him the result,' replied Nick.

'And what did he say?'

'Very little really, except something that somehow aptly expressed his nature.'

'And what was that?'

'He said, "Well done, Dancing Faun."'

CHAPTER NINE

The Fired Imagination

IF ENOUGH PASSION or interest is invested in an artist and his work, the chances of discovering a hitherto unknown work by them increase enormously. A rationalist would argue that this is because the finder is attuned, and thus more apt to notice what he would otherwise pass by, but why should there not be something divine or supernatural at work? The coincidence is sometimes so great, the synchronicity so faultlessly neat, that there appears to be no other satisfactory answer. I had serious reason to consider this five years ago.

In 1986 I had been making a television series on the history of British portrait painting, and for the programme concerned with the 18th century had ended up at Gainsborough House – the artist's birthplace in Sudbury, Suffolk which is now a museum devoted to his work. In order to explain the origins of the artist and his style, I was talking about a painting of a young boy considered to be the teenage painter's earliest known, formal portrait, and which the museum had bought at Christie's a number of years earlier (*Fig. 40*). 'The tragedy of this portrait,' I remember saying to the camera, 'is that it has been cut in half:

the girl who once sat next to this boy is now lost, and only known through the remnants of a dress.'

It was a disastrous day for filming; we kept on being interrupted by extraneous noises of tramping feet and passing lorries, and I was regularly hashing my lines. I attempted to phrase the words 'perhaps we will find her' about ten times until finally, in despair, the director settled for the last take and called it a day – I cannot now remember what form the edited result took.

Those repeated lines of script with their implicit plea, which so exasperated us all that day, may not have been wasted after all, for just under two years later the young girl reappeared at Sotheby's – as a head-and-shoulder portrait. It had been mis-catalogued as the work of George Beare, a lesser-known portrait painter of the generation before Gainsborough, and had been consigned for sale from Edinburgh by the executor of a family estate; no details of its earlier provenance were known. Alas, by this time the young girl had been divested of her skirt, together with much of the rest of the composition. But that it was the lost girl there could be no doubt: not only was there an unmistakable stylistic link in the treatment of the features, but other shared elements – the blue of the dress, the wild flowers and barley, the other background branches – all indicated that she had once been joined to the young boy. I purchased it for a few thousand pounds and sold it to Gainsborough House museum, where the girl is now reunited with her companion, most probably her brother.

Thinking back to those embarrassingly and publicly repeated lines about the girl's potential re-emergence, and the extraordinarily remote chance, two years later, of her doing so; the fact that she had made her way across Britain, to the auction house over the road from where I work; the auction house's decision to include and illustrate the picture in a catalogue I would then see; and the way that I was predisposed to be able to recognise it – it all seems too perfectly synchronised merely to put down to chance.

Why should not finds of this kind have something to do with the spiritual presence of the artist – a symbiotic relationship that rewards the faithful dealer and increases the painter's posthumous reputation? There is undoubtedly a link between discovery and loyal service, and whilst preparing to write this last chapter, I came across a dramatic example that fully exemplifies the phenomenon. The man who made this particular discovery, just months before this book went to press, is a specialist in and devotee of Victorian art called Rupert Maas.

Rupert is part of the new generation of West End dealers. Physically, he is taller and stronger than the rest of us, possessed of limitless energy that can border on the frenetic, and he enjoys metal-welding in his spare time. He has a voracious and scholarly appetite for 19th-century British art, and took control of the family business in 1993 when he was 33, following in the footsteps of his father, Jeremy, who almost single-handedly invented the idea of selling then unfashionable Victorian paintings in the 1960s and early '70s. His gallery is located near where I work, just off New Bond Street, in London.

There is a figure in Rupert's life who from a young age captured his imagination – partly in response to a Victorian portrait photograph by Julia Margaret Cameron, first shown to him by his father when Rupert was a young teenager (*Fig. 42*). His name is Sir Coutts Lindsay, Bart (1824–1913). Rupert's interest derived partly from Sir Coutts's romantic appearance: he was regarded by many contemporaries as the most handsome man in London, rivalled only by another young blood of the period called Cyril Flower. He was tall and elegant, with an easy aristocratic charm that had a Byronic effect on young women – he had countless mistresses and a number of illegitimate children. Even his mother regarded him with uneasy awe: 'He is very kind and affectionate in manner, but he keeps me in constant terror,' she wrote to a

friend. 'If he were not my son, I should think him quite delight-
ful.' What set him apart from the average aristocratic rake, and
quite alarmed his mother, was his bohemian energy. He was one
of the pivotal figures in the Aesthetic movement, a group of
like-minded artists who sought to overturn the lugubrious
character of much of Victorian art and society in favour of a more
romantic and spiritual alternative, as exemplified by the works
of Whistler and the pre-Raphaelite Burne-Jones. 'Unlike most
modern aristocratic men about town,' Rupert points out, 'what
made him so interesting was an overriding passion for art.' Sir
Coutts was forever travelling to Italy for inspiration, and painted
a considerable amount himself, but his biggest contribution was
in founding the Grosvenor Gallery which provided the first serious alternative to the Royal Academy as a place to exhibit the
best of contemporary art. Very soon it rivalled the Academy in
popularity.

Sir Coutts started the Gallery in partnership with two others,
buying the building with his own and his wife Blanche's money.
It was located on the corner of Grosvenor Street and New Bond
Street in Mayfair, London, and opened on 1st May 1877. Not
to be present at its openings was considered social death, and
over 7,000 people came through the doors in the first year.
Thanks to a generator in the basement, the novel device of electric
light was used to show the artists' work, which included Burne-
Jones and Whistler themselves – the latter exhibiting his abstract
picture 'Nocturne in Black and Gold: Falling Rocket', which
caused the outraged critic John Ruskin to call him a 'coxcomb'
and accuse him of flinging 'a paint-pot in the public's face'. The
celebrated libel action ensued in which Whistler was awarded
a farthing's damages. Within this jostling, controversial and
electrically lit environment, Sir Coutts also displayed his own
paintings.

'What made him even more intriguing to me,' says Rupert,
'was that although in all he publicly exhibited sixty-seven pic-

tures, not one finished oil painting is known today.' For a man at the centre of London's art world this is fairly extraordinary. Furthermore, apart from some photographs and a handful of sketches and watercolours, neither Rupert nor Sir Coutts's biographers had been able to find any formal portraits of him as an adult either. The lack of paintings by Sir Coutts may have been partly explained by the fact that his wife, whom he married in his late eighties, was impoverished after his death and may have been obliged to sell them off; but it certainly did not explain why not even one was known today. The complete absence of any significant paintings either of him or by him seemed to Rupert tantamount to a conspiracy. Some years earlier, Rupert and his father had bought and sold a five-leaf screen that had belonged to the Lindsay family, comprising a collage of drawings by all the family. There were a very few drawings by Sir Coutts amongst these but that was more or less the sum of Rupert's, and for that matter the art world's visual knowledge of his work. The lack of physical evidence for a man Rupert saw as one of the central figures in late-19th-century British art only further increased his fascination, adding a dimension of mystery to Sir Coutts's aura. His deep-rooted fascination in Sir Coutts, intensified by a biography by Virginia Surtees (*Coutts Lindsay 1824–1913*, 1993) which he avidly read, gave Rupert an ardent desire to rectify the situation.

It was an averagely frantic morning at the gallery and Rupert picked up the latest Sotheby's New York Arcade catalogue for a sale in two weeks' time, hastening to get through it and move on to more pressing things. The Arcade sales are for the lower-quality items which the New York auction house deems of insufficient status to include in their major sales, and they are normally crammed with lots. This time there were over six hundred pictures, almost all illustrated, and Rupert raced over the pages with a dismissive but professional eye. Towards the middle, as he was beginning to tire, his eye suddenly stopped on a small black-and-white reproduction of a painting showing an artist seated before an easel, palette in hand. 'I bet you that's Sir Coutts Lindsay,' Rupert said to his colleague, Fiona Halpin. She looked over to the catalogue and read the description. The illustration was no more than $1\frac{1}{2} \times 2$ inches and beneath it were the words, 'British School circa 1860, Seated Artist, 30×36 inches, oil on panel, estimate: \$800–\$1,200.'

Both telephone lines then rang, a customer came through the door, Rupert was late for an appointment, and the picture was set aside.

Three mornings later Rupert was in his bath. It is a daily experience he prolongs for as long as possible, for his baths are rare moments of stationary reflection in a life lived at breakneck pace. The image of the Sotheby's picture returned to him, much as one might suddenly recall a sequence from a dream of some days before. 'It was almost as if it had taken three days to filter through,' Rupert recalls. Although the image had triggered a response in Rupert when he had first seen it, there had not been the opportunity for him to process it, at least not consciously. It *had* looked like Sir Coutts, he now thought, and furthermore, why had he not considered that it could also be a self-portrait: a 'double whammy' in other words – the only known formal oil painting of him and by him. He was astonished at the delay in his own responses, and in a mood of Archimedean excitement he leapt from the water, bade goodbye to his wife and baby, and made for the gallery.

He looked at the illustration again. It was smaller than he remembered but, taking it into the daylight, he now fiercely rallied his concentration. Sure enough, he thought, that was him all right – the rakish, aristocratic features compared exactly with the photograph by Julia Margaret Cameron, particularly in this languid, casual pose which fitted what Rupert knew of Sir Coutts so well. He then reread the catalogue description of the picture and was reminded that it was painted on panel. This was a most unusual support for a Victorian picture – they are usually on canvas – but perhaps not so strange for a man like Sir Coutts. Enamoured of Italy, his favourite stamping-ground, perhaps he was attempting to emulate early Italian painting, which was almost always executed on wood – a sophisticated conceit which would have been typical of Coutts. Next Rupert tried to assess the painting technique. Sir Coutts's close friend was the eminent painter George Frederick Watts, and examining the loose but highly worked brush-strokes in the curtains and furniture it now reminded Rupert of that painter's style. If Sir Coutts was going to reveal the influence of another contemporary painter in his work, he reflected, Watts would be a more likely choice than most. Rupert then looked behind the sitter, through his studio window, and into the landscape. The skyline curved steeply upwards to the right, suggesting a mountain. Sir Coutts lived at Balcarres in Fife, and the backdrop, although not overly specific, could easily be a Scottish vista.

The illustration was too small to make any further deductions, so that afternoon Rupert rang the auction house in New York and asked them to send him photographs of some of the forthcoming lots, amongst them the one of the artist in his studio. By ordering a number of photographs in this way he would disguise his specific interest in the one lot, which he hoped he would be able to see in more detail from a larger photograph.

Nicolas Barker, the author of a book on the famous Lindsay library, and whom Rupert knew as a friend, was the person he rang next. 'Would you be able to recognise a portrait of Sir Coutts Lindsay from a black-and-white illustration one inch by two?' he asked Nicolas.

'Certainly,' he replied, and came over to the gallery that same afternoon on the bicycle which he uses to travel everywhere. Barker took one look and was in complete agreement: the unmistakable features combined with the other elements in the picture to fit his perception of Sir Coutts exactly.

'I did nothing till the photograph arrived,' says Rupert. 'In the absence of any other comparative works, there was little more I could do to enhance the case.' The black-and-white picture that arrived later that week was three times the size of the catalogue illustration, and brought with it three more clues. Behind the artist's chair was a piece of armour: Sir Coutts possessed a large collection of armour and there was actually a photograph of him dressed up in a breastplate! Rupert was now also able to make out that an object leaning against the figure's chair was a portfolio of drawings. Barker pointed out that Sir Coutts is recorded as having produced numerous watercolour sketches on his trips to Italy (some of which had been glued to the screen Rupert had sold) and it seemed plausible that this side of his life was being referred to here. Most revealing of all, however, Rupert could now see the picture which hung on the wall within the picture in greater detail. It seemed to portray a dark hooded figure in a wood clasping a child. Keeping this image in mind, he then went through the written descriptions of all Sir Coutts's exhibited pictures in an attempt to find one that matched it. There were sixty-seven to choose from, all described in records of exhibits held in the private library at Agnew's, and amongst them he found one that seemed to tally. It was described as 'A Knight and His Daughter', and had been exhibited at the Grosvenor Gallery in 1879. There was no more description than that, but looking again at the figure with a child, and bearing in mind other works of the period and the *vernacular* of historical portrayal, he felt that this could be the very same picture. But there was a small hitch. The portrait at auction seemed most likely to date from the early 1860s, and therefore if the picture-within-the-picture were the *same* as the one exhibited in 1879, that would mean that it had been painted some fifteen or so years *before* being shown in public. But that was not an uncommon occurrence for artists, particularly those who were not overly productive and who, in need of work at short notice for exhibition, would grab anything lying around in their studio.

With the benefit of the large photograph's improved clarity, Rupert was now also able to study the painter's technique more analytically. There were both strengths and weaknesses: surveying the composition as a whole, he noticed some areas of detail seemed better described than others. This, though, he reflected, was only to be expected as Sir Coutts was not a professional painter, and his lack of concentration had been noted. The painting had verve and confidence, particularly the languid pose, but perhaps lacked the understanding of anatomy that a master like Watts would have had. This all seemed consistent with what Rupert knew of Sir Coutts's character – the precocious, restless aesthete who valued vision over application. Rupert could also now see that the painting had the subtle but certain hallmark of a self-portrait – a concentrated gaze that combined vanity with seriousness of purpose. The right-angled pose and quarter turn of the head were also the signs of a painter recording himself with the use of a mirror.

Rupert left for New York a day before the sale. He was so charged with the excitement of the chase that he told a complete stranger in the seat next to him the whole story, how Sir Coutts had wooed his imagination as a boy, his father's photograph, the chance sighting of the picture and his subsequent deductions. 'Pretty imprudent, I suppose, but I was so excited it had to come out somehow. Far better to do it to a stranger than another art dealer!'

He entered the cavernous saleroom in the basement of Sotheby's and passed the rows of pictures – so numerous as to evoke a mediocre stamp collection: there are so many pictures in these lesser sales that the eyes become numbed. An art fair was taking place in Manhattan at the time, and because many of the London art dealers would present in the city, Rupert arrived early to avoid being seen. 'I hardly needed to glance twice at the

picture when I finally came across it,' Rupert told me, 'I could
see instantly that it was everything I had hoped for.' Two
thoughts came to him in quick succession. The first was that he
was now a hundred per cent sure that this was not only Sir
Coutts, but a self-portrait as well. He had needed to see the
picture itself for this intuitive response to be utterly satisfied,
but now that he was standing before the painted panel its nature
communicated itself powerfully. The second was that he liked
it. With discoveries, there is a tendency to lose the normal
faculties of objective assessment and judgement, and to become
blinded by excitement and self-congratulation. But reining in
the euphoria and summoning his dispassionate powers of observation, he now appreciated that it was also a good picture – in
art-dealing terms it was well enough painted, and attractive
enough to be commercial as an object in its own right, whatever
the subject or artist. It was also far dirtier than he had imagined,
and he forecast that it would clean dramatically.

'So what are you going to go up to?' asked Nicolas Barker.
Rupert had telephoned him with his reactions later that morning.
'$80,000, I think,' replied Rupert, 'perhaps more. I shall bid
myself.' He was now determined, almost come what may, that he
was going to return home with the picture. Rupert had originally
intended to get a non-art-dealing friend to bid for him, but on
reflection felt that his friend's lack of experience in bidding,
coupled with the fact that he had noticed Sotheby's were inclined
to use their less experienced auctioneers in these lesser sales,
might result in catastrophe. What if the bid were missed by an
new auctioneer who failed to notice an amateur bidder? It would
be unthinkable to lose his picture in this way after the hope and
endeavour he had invested.

This meant executing the bid himself. But it concerned him
that if he himself were seen to be bidding in a minor sale – a
trader known to the art world as a dealer with academic knowledge in Victorian pictures – it might encourage unnecessary

competition from rivals thinking that he was on to something exciting. It is the sort of prudence any serious dealer would consider. But that would be a risk he would now have to take.

'It was just as well,' he told me, 'the lots were sold very fast, sometimes they were missed out, and from what I can recall there were three or four changeovers of auctioneers.' The lot number was 148, and at the sale's rattling pace, it came up mercifully fast. Rupert raised his hand at $800, and another bidder at the far end of the room then took it a bid higher. He did not recognise the face, and guessed that it might be an American dealer on the scent of an attractive artefact for stock, probably unaware of the picture's deeper significance. The price then rose rapidly, at a far greater speed in fact than in more significant sales, where the amounts are larger, and the bidding more ponderous, and in no time Rupert found that he was being beckoned by the auctioneer to raise his bid to $2,500. Whoever he is, that dealer wants it, thought Rupert, and nodded back to the auctioneer in compliance. To go a further bid, the competition would have to take it to $2,600, which would mean touching $3,000 with 15 per cent buyer's commission – a psychological cut-off point for the uncommitted.

It did the trick, the underbidder dropped out, and the auctioneer surveyed the crowd for more offers. Rupert looked around anxiously for the familiar faces of rival dealers, and over to the telephones for absentee British bidders about to enter the fray from their armchairs across the Atlantic. But the room seemed unconcerned, the telephone bidders looked bored. 'I'm selling at $2,500,' called out the auctioneer. Rupert kept his gaze locked on the auctioneer, and after a further second's pause, watched him crack down the gavel: 'I had to resist the urge to jump for joy,' says Rupert. Sir Coutts by Sir Coutts has now returned home – and is in the possession of his great admirer (*Fig. 41*).

* * *

Rupert did not know of the existence of a self-portrait of Sir Coutts, the subject of his interest and high regard, until he found it. But the process of 'summoning' can also happen when you have a fair, if not exact, notion of what you are looking for. With the Gainsborough's 'other half', I knew of its possible existence and likely appearance. But in the case of an amazing turn-up in 1978, the discoverers had an even more highly developed notion of what they were looking for. The story involves two people who have already featured in this book, but this time at the outset of their respective careers: Richard Knight, the restorer/dealer who now heads up Colnaghi's and who was then dealing on his own; and David Dallas, the man who (nearly) found the Strozzi flower piece and who at the time of this story had just started up a gallery on his own, with financial backing from a friend of his father. Dave and Richard were the same age, they had both trained at Phillips, they were close friends and were now forging a way in the art business under separate banners. Richard was perpetually on the road in his red Vauxhall estate, returning to London with barrowloads of art purchased from country antique shops and galleries, whilst Dave was more usually in London, covering the sales and looking after his new gallery. Both look back with evident nostalgia to the time when, as young bucks in a market that offered more buying scope than it does now, they were perpetually hunting, acquiring, reselling, researching and promoting pictures that would now no longer be so affordable. It was before the heady days of the '80s when the price of art increased disproportionately, it seemed, in relation to everything else – a time when the stakes were lower and buying opportunities greater.

The *Burlington Magazine* was then, as now, the most important publication in the academic and commercial art world. First published in London, in March 1903, it provides an international forum for discussion and the latest scholarship in the applied arts. With a strength in old masters, its contributors are often academics, as are the editorial staff. In many ways it is the academic backbone of the profession – attempting to present the latest findings with strenuous objectivity, and to be found on the reading tables of galleries and museums and the more serious commercial art dealers.

The ambitious young Richard Knight read the monthly publications with interest, and there was one subject in particular that had imprinted itself deeply on his imagination. It concerned a painter called Adam Elsheimer, an important German artist who was working in Rome at the turn of the 16th century. He died when he was only thirty-two and left a legacy of barely more than thirty works, but all are highly regarded by modern art historians for their exquisite colouring and design. The articles which Richard had read were to do with one particular work by Elsheimer, probably his most celebrated, an altarpiece commissioned by the Grand Duke of Tuscany in 1619 depicting (in separate panels) scenes from the Finding of the True Cross – a post-New Testament subject occasionally found in Renaissance art. There was, however, a major problem with this work: until 1952 it was only known from the original drawings and from letters between the artist and patron that had survived in manuscript form in the Medici Archive in Florence. For the magnificent object, with its seven separate panels, had been broken up and lost at some time in its history, and the series of articles in the *Burlington* that so inspired Richard had chartered the emergence and coming together of some of these panels over the previous twenty-five years. In 1952 the first panel was recognised by Christie's. It came in as a picture by an unknown artist that had long been in the collection of the Duke of Norfolk, and they soon identified it as the central panel of the missing altarpiece: 'The Exaltation of the Cross'. Appropriately, it was purchased by the Stadelsches Kunstinstitut Museum of Frankfurt, Elsheimer's home town and seemed to open the floodgates. In 1955 a picture in the collection of Sir Alec Martin was identified as one of the wings, and via Colnaghi's was sent to join the central panel in Frankfurt. In 1970, the other wing, entitled the 'Embarkation of St Helena', was found in a private house in Ireland. A year later two of the panels came up for sale at Christie's – the owner had found them in an outhouse at his family home and took them along to Christie's to see if they would raise any funds. They were identified as two of the four lower predella panels and the pair subsequently sold for over £50,000 to the same museum.

This left two panels to find and Richard, inspired and fascinated by the account, longed to find them. He carefully studied the illustrations of the recent finds, and later went to the Frankfurt museum. 'The atmosphere of that intimate room,' he recalls, 'was so special and magical that it left a lasting impression. The altarpiece was an unforgettable work of art.' The eminent London frame-maker, Paul Levi, had been commissioned to make the altarpiece's surround, from existing drawings of the original, and thus it stood in the museum, five of its sockets replete with images, and two from the lower row hollow and expectant, awaiting the next gifts of destiny (*Fig. 43*).

A regular viewer of the London sales, Dave was checking out Bonhams. The auction was full of old-master pictures of varying quality, but it was not so much what was on the walls that interested him but a glass case, where the smaller, and sometimes more precious lots were housed. One little painting irritated him, not because of what it portrayed, or how it was painted, but purely because it struck a chord and he couldn't get it out of his mind. He returned to the saleroom three times, and with each encounter the feeling became stronger. What particularly intrigued him was the painting's support: it was on copper that had been silver-plated under the painted side giving the composition, though partly obscured by grime, a tarnished resonance. It was no bigger than the palm of his hand, and the figures shone like enamel: a youth lifting himself up from a cross, surrounded by six onlooking figures including a mitred cleric and a turbaned Jewish official, in a scene which David did not immediately recognise. What he did recognise, however, was its masterful colouring and design, and he could not rid it from his mind. It also reminded him of something he had seen recently, but could not place. The lot was catalogued as 'Italian School, 17th century', given an estimate of £200–£300 and David felt sure that Richard would not only appreciate it, but might also be able to work out more about it.

David had been pestering Richard to view the painting ever since he had first seen it, but despite his constant peregrinations around the Home Counties he had been unable to find the time to go one mile to Knightsbridge. 'Let's both go now, and you'll see what I mean,' wheedled David, and there and then they drove to the auction rooms at Montpelier Street. As Richard neared the glass case and saw the painting he whispered to Dave, 'When you turn the panel over you will see the inscription, in the artist's hand, his own handwriting.' Richard seemed transfixed. Dave asked for a porter to open the case and then turned back to Richard whose gaze was still locked on the little picture. Slowly Richard turned to Dave and silently mouthed, 'Adam Elsheimer' and then added, 'it has to be one of them' (*Fig. 44*).

It all rushed back to David in a split second. He too had read the article, the painting had stirred something in his memory, but it had been his intuition that carried him this far. It all crashed into place and at last he fully understood Richard's mesmeric response. David lifted the panel out of the case and did as Richard had suggested, turning it over and looking deeply into the copper's tarnished patina for evidence of writing. Almost completely disguised, and in parts rubbed away, they then both began to make out some words of script. It was too illegible to decipher but was undoubtedly what Richard was looking for – Elsheimer's inscription of the subject, which Richard knew was also on the other panels in the altarpiece at Frankfurt, labelling the different stages in the narrative. This particular scene showed Judas's attempt to discover which of three crosses that had been dug up was the true one, as opposed to those used for the criminals, by placing them, one at a time, on the corpse of a young man on its way to be buried. This was the moment of drama when the true one, upon which Christ had died, had been placed upon the man, raising him from the dead.

They returned to Dave's gallery and, having quelled their excitement, turned to the practicalities. This was one of the few occasions when they could rely on an utterly captive client, the Stadelsches Kunstinstitut in Frankfurt who were ready and waiting for the next two panels in the altarpiece to turn up. As long as they were fair, in other words not too greedy, there was an excellent profit to be had. But the very information that had allowed them to recognise the panels – the articles in the *Burlington* – was also their bane for if *they* had both read the pieces and reacted so strongly, surely others would also have done? They were young dealers at the start of their careers and neither was equipped to fight it out over a few thousand pounds. On further reflection David decided he would go to his backer, his father's friend who was financing the gallery, and put the problem to him. If they expressed the likely up-side well enough, he might well be persuaded to risk the money himself. Richard completed the rest of the research, confirming that the picture's measurements of $5\frac{3}{4} \times 6\frac{1}{4}$ inches (14.7 × 16.2 cm) were consistent with the other panels in the predella, and Dave then made his case, with two days to go before the sale.

He came away from his backer with a bid of up to £30,000 in return for a substantial share of the profit. This should be ample, they thought, to knock out most of the heavier guns, should they have a go, but if one of the major players with infinite means were to enter the contest, it would probably count for nothing. They worked out that they could sell the panel for up to £50,000 or £60,000, bearing in mind the prices achieved for the others and the inevitable desire of the museum to make their altarpiece complete.

'I remember we stood at the back,' says Richard, 'because Dave wanted to be near the loo. In any event the room was so crowded that there were no places to sit, and all I can remember was a sea of faces.' So there they stood in readiness, two young bloods in the first years of their business, prepared to execute a bid that they themselves could never normally afford but which, if successful, would represent a major triumph, both art-historically and commercially. This was a picture they had both dreamed about, particularly Richard, and it was now within reach.

'Hang on,' said Dave, 'what's he doing here?' Standing a few feet away was Paul Levi, the man who had been commissioned by the Stadelsches to make the frame for the altarpiece – the one man who could be guaranteed to know the panels and their history intimately and who they had rarely, if ever, noticed at an auction before. More shattering still was their recognition of the tall man standing near by: Jack Baer, of Hazlitt, Gooden & Fox, the heavyweight London art dealers who worked closely with Levi and commissioned many of his frames. 'Oh shit,' said Dave, turning to Richard for comfort. But Richard was now looking at the other corner of the room at a less familiar face, but one he had encountered before. It was Herr Bohler, an eminent second-generation Munich old-master dealer, who would never normally attend a sale of this stature, but who was now standing there, catalogue in hand, amidst the dense group of standing dealers.

'We never even got our hand up,' Dave recalls. The two titans, both fully aware of the small panel's commercial potential reduced the room to silent awe with the ferocity of their intent. The bidding started at £200, quickly rising to £5,000, at which point all faces in the room turned to the buyers. They fought on, but at £50,000 Herr Bohler declined to go any further, and

Paul Levi, bidding on behalf of Jack Baer, then purchased the panel. He later sold it on to the Stadelsches for an undisclosed price. It was, in fact, a classic case of a sleeper which found its own level in the market place, despite being missed by the auction house.

Dave and Richard have gone on to make many more discoveries in their lives, but will never forget those astonishing three days at the outset of their careers when so important a picture, which had been in their thoughts even before its emergence, so accommodatingly reappeared. They did not go home entirely without consolation, however. Another picture, by Honthorst, of an old lady removing lice from a prostitute's hair and catalogued simply as 'North Italian School', was spotted by Richard. He bought it, and they later sold it, making a handsome return.

Some months afterwards the last of the panels was found. It had lain unrecognised at the Wellcome Institute for Medical Studies in London – appropriately enough, for the subject showed St Elizabeth feeding the sick – and it, too, made its way to Frankfurt. The altarpiece is now complete (*Fig. 45*). 'We found out sometime afterwards,' says Dave, 'what the title of the picture was that we couldn't read at the time. Quite appropriate really: "*Quando la trovarono*" – "When they found it".'

The moral of the story is that this mysterious magnetism which draws the finder to his heart's desire is not enough on its own: it needs help. Dave and Richard had neither the funds nor, perhaps, the experience in dealing to compete with the formidable established traders. But even the established, on occasions, are obliged to resort to unorthodox means to complete the process of discovery. The most touching tale of an object being 'summoned' that I have encountered involves one of the patriarchs of the business, Rupert Maas's father, Jeremy, resorting to 'benign subterfuge' in order to finish the work that the fairies had begun.

Although now retired, Jeremy is unquestionably one of the founders of the modern art business. He delighted in a period that at the time nobody cared much for – Victorian England – defined the main artists, wrote books about them, and established a business to sell their works. In the 1960s he helped to both create the demand and provide the supply in formerly ridiculed subjects like the pre-Raphaelites and 19th-century Victorian neo-classical painters.

He is now retired and living in Sussex, but occasionally returns to the world of commerce to help Rupert at art fairs. He is so intimately acquainted with the Victorian artists he writes about that he speaks of them as if they were schoolfriends, occasionally critically, more often enthusiastically, and always with the authority of someone deeply familiar with their traits.

One artist who has always intrigued him is John Anster Fitzgerald. He was known in the 1850s as 'Fairy Fitzgerald' for his overriding preoccupation with fairy subjects, an eccentric aside to mainstream Victorian painting in which he excelled. Only about twenty oil paintings are known, together with a fair number of watercolours, but his masterly rendering of imps, goblins, fairies and other creatures from his imagination, integrated into exquisite studies of nature and painted in iridescent pre-Raphaelite colouring, turned him into the Rembrandt of this idiosyncratic genre. Today, in a competitive collectors' market, his little oil paintings could make anything up to £100,000.

When a runner arrived at Jeremy's gallery in 1965 offering him not one, but two oil paintings by the artist he could hardly believe his good fortune. The only problem, he recalls, was that the runner was 'a very, very, unpleasant man'. His charmlessness was not redeemed by his business practices either, and having obtained an offer of £500 from Jeremy, he then touted them to other galleries along Bond Street, received increased offers, and returned to Jeremy to improve on them. This Dutch auction continued, and although Jeremy would not normally participate in this reprehensible bartering process – it is not considered decent business practice between professionals – he was so enamoured of the little paintings that he forwent his normal reserve: 'It was a case of plucking a rose from a dungheap,' he recalled, 'and in the end I succeeded in acquiring them for £800.' But despite their unsavoury provenance he was now delighted to be their new owner for a price that was not out of the way at the time.

They were both small (10 × 12 inches) and showed two different fantasies with similar components: one of fairies having a giant banquet around a mushroom and the other a moonlit scene of three beautiful androgens in a bird's nest surrounded by fairy people. Neither had frames, which was a serious drawback as normal picture surrounds look ludicrously clumsy around such intimate and fantastic feats of imagination. Jeremy took the pictures home to enjoy himself, as unframed but bewitching objects which appealed deeply to his taste for Victorian eccentricity. A couple of years later he needed to raise funds to re-decorate his house and so sold the mushroom banquet for a few thousand pounds. It was a wrench, but he marginally preferred the other picture, and was content to have a single and outstanding example of Fitzgerald's work in a home that was decorated to match. He had been unable to find a frame that suited it even remotely, and so it remained, a glorious but incomplete artefact.

A year or so later, Jeremy went to visit the home of a good friend, John Rickett, who in those days managed the entire picture department at Sotheby's. Passing through his downstairs cloakroom he then stopped dead in his tracks. Hanging on a coat peg from a piece of string was what looked at first glance like a square bird's nest. On closer inspection it turned out to be an elaborate little frame, 'I could hardly believe my eyes,' he recalled, 'straight away I knew it had to be the frame from my picture.' Its dimensions and idiosyncrasies left him in no doubt whatsoever. It consisted of an intricate mesh of gilded twigs that sprouted organically from a knobbly, rectangular construct, into which could fit a picture. 'It was as if it had been summoned

out of the ether – there it hung, just waiting for me to find it.'
Not only would this make his little image complete, Jeremy
thought, but as something obviously designed for the picture by
the artist it would double its value as well. 'I did not even feel
the need to try it around the picture, so certain was I that this
had to be its missing surround.'

'Where on earth did you find that extraordinary object,' he
said to John when he went back upstairs. He knew John well,
they had done much auction business together, and Jeremy was
mindful that he could be competitive and might react mischiev-
ously if he knew Jeremy wanted something badly! He therefore
concealed his full agenda and expressed his interest in the surround as a quirky object rather than the missing part of his
prized picture.

John happily recounted the story. A dealer had recently called
round to show him a picture. It was a small 17th-century German
old master of average merit, but it was not helped by its extraordinary frame which dated from a few hundred years later.
Instead of a conventional wooden frame which would have suited
a composition of that nationality and date, it had this elaborate
composition of twigs – the bird's-nest frame – which was dramatically at odds with the picture's character. John was intrigued
by the frame all the same, and asked the dealer if he would like
him to find one that better suited his picture, and to give him
the bird's nest in exchange. The dealer agreed, he found him a
new frame, and John thereby ended up with this bizarre item,
for which he had no proper use, except ornamental.

Try as he might, however, Jeremy could not get his friend to
sell it. With Jeremy's growing exhortations he only became more
intransigent, and thus he had to leave it – his picture at home
crying out for completion, and its miraculously reappeared companion frame hanging tantalizingly from a string in John's downstairs cloakroom.

'Shortly afterwards, John tragically died,' said Jeremy, 'and for a time I forgot all about the frame.' A year later, however, he telephoned John's widow, Alys. She had been disposing of some of her husband's pictures, and so he now put it to her that she might consider selling him the frame from the cloakroom. But for whatever reason she felt disinclined to do so, and Jeremy began to feel that picture and frame were destined to remain for ever asunder. How unjust, he thought, having come so close to benefiting from such an extraordinary quirk of destiny, for it to remain out of his grasp.

A few months later he received a telephone call from Alys. She needed a valuation of her husband's pictures for probate and asked Jeremy if he would mind taking it on. 'With pleasure,' and he would of course make no charge for this service to his deceased friend and his widow. Having performed the task, he then sent Alys the written report and enclosed with it an invoice. 'It was one of those clerical errors that sort of happen on purpose,' he told me with a gleeful smile. She rang him the following morning.

'Jeremy, Jeremy, I need to speak to you,' she cried. 'I am so sorry, Alys,' said Jeremy, seizing the initiative, 'we sent you a standard invoice.' Before he went through the motions of apologising and telling her to ignore the bill, she added, unprompted: 'You can have the frame; you can have it, Jeremy!'

And so, with a gentle twist of the arm, Jeremy was able to reunite the fairies with their rightful home. 'The extraordinary thing was that it fitted utterly. Not only would it go in only one way, but the twigs parted at exactly the right spot to reveal Fitzgerald's signature.' Two of the twigs in the picture – in the bottom left-hand corner, and just above the middle of the right-hand side – were continued in the twigs of the frame, indicating the extraordinary degree to which it had been designed as a whole (*Fig. 46*). And thus the picture remains today on Jeremy's wall, an example of the magnetism that can occur in our business – particularly when encouraged.

It also serves as an important reminder about *all* the discoveries in this book. I may, on occasions, have given the impression that events and destiny have behaved unusually well when required to: that lost masterpieces appear too easily when summoned, vital pieces of evidence too willingly when needed. But fortune requires more than just a prepared mind. All the attributes of the hunter – tenacity, determination, stamina, hunger and even mild aggression – are vital in this game too. They are the less glamorous, but critical qualities of the discoverer, enabling him not only to wake up, but to bring home the sleeper. Together with connoisseurship, they are characteristic of most of the people featured in these pages, the warrior-class of professionals who have chosen the art world, rather than any other, as the arena in which to exercise their particular strengths. In combination with the extraordinary circumstances described in this book, they have achieved some memorable results.

Index

INDEX